FASHION FENG SHUI FOR LIFE

Real-World Solutions for Finding Fulfillment and Prosperity

Carmen Okabe
Sue Donnelly, Anita Marie Bangerter, Else Gammergaard Madsen,
Andrea Dupont, Carol Parker Walsh, Stefania Rolandelli,
Beverley Eve Cole, Sabine Kaufmann, Lola Intagliata Avgoustatos,
Cindy Nytko, Cinzia Fassetta

Carmen Okabe and Andrew Maggiore, Editors

First Edition: April 2017
ISBN: 1545260524
ISBN-13: 978-1545260524
Printed in the United States

This book is available at special quantity discounts for bulk purchase for sales promotions, premiums, fundraising and educational needs. For details, write to sales@fashionfengshui.com.

Cover design concept by Carmen Okabe.
Layout by Too Fabulous For Words.

We dedicate this book to you…

You, the curious reader about fashion and about Feng Shui,
wondering what the marriage of the two will bring you.

You, the fashionista who loves colors.

You, who are still searching for your path, in life and in business.

You, who want to transform your look and feel good with the new you.

You, the image professional or coach in need
of a complete tool for your clients.

You, the parent, for learning how to look differently at your children.

You, the lover, for knowing how to keep your love forever.

You, the one wanting to serve with your heart.

You, the believer in magic.

~ The Co-Authors of *Fashion Feng Shui for Life*

Contents

Acknowledgments

Every project needs a team in order to become reality, and this book is no exception. Before you start reading, please let us express our gratitude to a few people whose work made all this possible. We hail from eight countries across three continents, so the team assisting us had to be very international as well!

This book is the concept of Carmen Okabe, Romanian-Swiss Fashion Feng Shui® Master Facilitator and international consultant. She brought us together, inspiring us to share our feelings, experiences and knowledge about Fashion Feng Shui® with you. Her commitment to excellence, attention to detail, persuasive nature and active spirit contributed to the realization of this book that we all are so proud of.

We are truly grateful

To Karina Hof, who worked her linguistic magic to make our articles read correctly and coherently.

To Jeremy Hayes, who put his amazing design skills to work, giving shape and color to our chapters.

To Ioana Tanase, who assisted Carmen throughout the project and worked with each of us to give you our very best.

To Hassan Ahmad, CEO of Activation Sources Pakistan, who understood perfectly what we had in mind for a cover and made it something really wonderful.

And of course to Evana Maggiore, our beloved mentor, who was with us throughout this endeavor and gave us strength and inspiration from above. We hope we made you proud!

With gratitude, the Co-Authors of *Fashion Feng Shui for Life*

Foreword

By Carmen Okabe

The vision of this book came to me in a dream, in which Evana Maggiore, our beloved mentor and the initiator of Fashion Feng Shui®, was reminding me of my role in this life: connecting people and building bridges between different cultures. She was reminding me of our long discussions back in 2010, in London, when we were talking about the need to spread the word about Fashion Feng Shui® and create a "family" of facilitators, giving people the tools and knowledge for positive transformation.

This book is not just about Feng Shui, nor is it just about fashion. It is about building bridges with Fashion Feng Shui®, and using five-element theory to live it even better. Our 12 authors used their rich experiences and diverse backgrounds to craft the tapestry of this book: it contains our heart and soul, our colors, our desires, and of course the solutions we discovered and now offer to you.

This book will help you get to know yourself better and allow you to progress in various life situations. Your looks will go hand in hand with healing your soul, relating to your peers, building your brand or providing the very best service to your clients. I am thankful to the universe for allowing me to hear Evana's words, and for the power to realize this book, as a bridge between the authors and all of you. I hope you will enjoy our book and keep it with you for years to come. It can really change your life, just as Fashion Feng Shui® has changed ours!

From "Woo Woo" to "Wow"
Change Your Clothes, Change Your Life

By Sue Donnelly

It's pretty obvious that **the** most important aspect of Fashion Feng Shui® is how you pronounce it! Tongue in cheek, I know, but when I first began this part of my career, back in 2005, "fung shooey," "feng shwee," "fengy shway" and the like tell you that very few people had heard of it in my part of the world. At best, it appeared to be image with an Eastern twist. At worst, some kind of "new age" gobbledygook that had no relevance to anyone living in central England.

This book, and this chapter in particular, will put the record straight. It will show you just how influential Fashion Feng Shui® really is today. How, in a world that changes at the speed of a keystroke, it can promote confidence, self-esteem and authenticity in those that follow its teachings. It can positively change your life as it certainly did with mine.

Back to basics

The art of Feng Shui (pronounced *fung shway*), a tradition spanning more than 4,000 years, translates in its literal sense as "wind and water." The combination of these two powerful elements affects many aspects of our lives due to changes in the tide, our climate and our environment. It is concerned with creating a flow of energies between nature and mankind, bringing us into harmony and balance. In this way lies inner peace.

Feng Shui is also used in the healing process. Chi (pronounced *chee*), the "breath force" of energy, is the combination of wind and water, radiating through and into everything living, despite being invisible to the eye. Traditional Chinese acupuncture and shiatsu massage are two practices that unblock chi stuck within the body to promote physical, and psychological, health and wellness.

Most people think of Feng Shui in terms of a work or a home environment. Early cultures understood the importance of object placement to encourage the flow of chi or energy throughout their living space. It is still significant today. I'm guessing many of us have read about how moving a plant or creating a water feature, for instance, can encourage money, love or other positive outcomes into the household.

Fashion Feng Shui® takes the premise one step further, believing clothing is your body's most intimate environment. After all, unless you're a naturist, you get dressed every day. As everything, animate or inanimate, has its own energy, what you choose to wear will influence your life, whether or not you are aware of it. Fashion Feng Shui® teaches us to dress the **whole** person, the culmination of mind, body and spirit, so not only do we look fabulous but we feel fulfilled, and we are fortified to go after what we truly desire in life. Sound good?

My story

It all began with a simple question. Someone asked me for my favorite color and there was no hesitation in my response "indigo." I love its rich, bold, decadence and always have. The qualities of sensuality, mystery and drama found in its purple inkiness fill me with pure joy. On answering, I realized something extremely profound. I owned no clothing in this color, nothing at all. No accessories, shoes, bags, nada. If I loved it so much, this didn't make any sense. Why wasn't it showing up, and prominently, in my wardrobe?

I had decided to become an image consultant a couple of years beforehand. My training primarily instructed me in how to analyze a person's individual coloring and body shape to provide a set of "rules" for them to follow. This would enable them to choose, more easily, garments that flattered their face and their body. In my role of consultant, it was crucial that I applied those same principles to my own attire; otherwise, I would be sure to lose my credibility.

Although I loved what I did, my first few years in the image industry had been fraught with confusion. The clothing I thought I *ought* to wear did not fit with what I *wanted* to wear. As a newly qualified professional, and a born people-pleaser, I desperately wanted to follow the rules and tried really hard to do so. Shopping for clothes had changed from something I had always loved to a chore. Continually checking color swatch books or putting garments back because the fabric, pattern, design, hemline or shape wasn't right took all the joy and playfulness out of an activity I had previously been passionate about. My innate instinct to choose clothes that suited both my personality and my mood had been quashed.

I was well aware of the importance of matching the color characteristics of depth, clarity and undertone to a person's complexion so he or she always looks radiant. However, in my case, the summer palette, best suited to my complexion consists mainly of pastels and soft tones. Indigo would be considered way too deep for my skin tone. Despite my misgivings, my closet was a rainbow of lilac, mauve, pale blue and pink. These soft colors did not represent how I felt about myself at all. I was a strong, dynamic woman with lots of character, not an elegant, gentle, more refined soul. The external me and the internal me were at odds with one another.

The answer came in the form of a wonderful teacher and mentor, the late and much-missed Evana Maggiore, the creator of Fashion Feng Shui®.

I had always thought, like most other people, that Feng Shui was applicable only to your home. In reality, our closet is the one place we go to every single day without fail. We choose clothes to suit an occasion, our lifestyle and our emotions. How many of us have swapped clothes because we're having a "fat day" or we want to feel powerful or in control at work?

How many of us have put on an outfit that seemed OK at the time, but ended up feeling miserable all day? The outfit hasn't changed—we have.

Fashion Feng Shui® is a technique that teaches people how to follow nature's master plan providing them with a personal style that is authentic, empowering and enhancing. During her study to become a Feng Shui Master, Evana realized that if a design element changed in a fabric so did the resulting energy. This affected the overall appearance, its purpose and its fundamental nature. Evana acknowledged that if this was true for home furnishings, it could also be true for the fabrics and designs we choose to put on our bodies. By manipulating the design elements of a garment she could adjust its energy, bringing harmony and balance to the wearer.

Over time, she came to the conclusion that clothing is the body's most intimate environment and therefore as influential on people's lives as are their personal and professional surroundings. She saw a pattern emerging. Body coloring, shape, style personality, lifestyle and goals aligned perfectly with the colors, shapes and substances of the five elements which, according to Eastern philosophy, make up the whole of life, connecting cosmic energy to physical form. Evana had discovered a new language, using the five elements, to describe an entire body of image industry techniques. That was back in 1996. Fashion Feng Shui® is now a global phenomenon with facilitators situated around the world.

The "F" words

Unlike most traditional image training, Fashion Feng Shui® encapsulates the mind, the body and the spirit so that we are dressing the whole person. Its aim is to create a wardrobe that is **fulfilling, fortifying, flattering** and **functional**. We call these the **"F" words**. I add a couple of my own personal F ones—**fabulous** and **fantastic**—because that's what it is.

Evana taught me how my **essence** was at the foundation of any successful closet. She showed me how emotions and spirit play such a large part in how we dress. If they did not, we would put on the same things every day without considering how we feel or what we look like. Unfortunately, the latter still applies to many people even now. They have a uniform that's unlikely to change, from fear of ridicule, lack of knowledge or just sheer laziness. But, the crux of the matter is this; what you wear is as influential on your life as how you decorate your home or your workspace. Dressing needs to be "mindful" (a buzzword today that Evana was already using years ago) and intentional so your clothes not only express who you are at your very core, but act as a magnet for what you most desire in your life.

What I love so much about Fashion Feng Shui® is how it tailors the five elements to **specifically suit each individual**. This means no one looks like anyone else. It works for everyone. You can make (and break) your own rules, so that what you wear makes you feel innovated, activated, stimulated, stabilized or refined.

How fantastic would that be for young girls beholden to the perfection of their (often digitally touched-up) Instagram heroines? Research in the UK has already shown that depression in our teenage girls is on the increase. One of the main reasons cited is their lack of confidence in how they look. The need to belong to a tribe, to look a certain way, to dress to conform, regardless of whether or not it suits them, can be hard to live with.

The five elements
Fashion Feng Shui®'s point of departure from other image practices is five-element theory, which is based on nature's most basic elements:
1. Water
2. Wood
3. Fire
4. Earth
5. Metal

Each element has specific characteristics that are unique in terms of color, shape and substance, and each is related to a time of day, time of year, organs in the body and the subsequent emotions attached.

Water

Dark colors
Flowing/wavy/asymmetric shapes and patterns
Fluid/reflective substances e.g. glass, sheer fabrics
Winter
Night
Bladder, ears, bones, head, hair and kidney—Fear

Wood

Blue/green
Vertical/columnar shapes and patterns
Plant-based substances e.g. denim, linen
Spring
Morning
Liver, eyes, nails and gall bladder—Anger

Fire

Red/purple
Diamond and triangular shapes and patterns
Light- or life-based substances e.g. flames, silk, fur
Summer
Noon
Heart, small intestine, pericardium—Joy

Earth

Brown/yellow/earth tones
Square shapes and patterns
Soil-based substances e.g. dirt, ceramic, wool
Late summer—harvest

Afternoon
Spleen, mouth, lips and stomach—Worry

Metal
Metallic/pastels/white
Oval and rounded shapes and patterns
Ore-based substances e.g. steel, gemstones, metals
Autumn
Evening
Large intestine, skin and lungs—Grief/sorrow

The elemental archetypes

Fashion Feng Shui® "personifies" these five elements as five different elemental archetypes. Each have their own core values (essence),
preferences & goals (intention) and the elements of physical & clothing
design (appearance).

Water—The Philosopher
Wood—The Pioneer
Fire—The Pleasure Seeker
Earth—The Peacemaker
Metal—The Perfectionist

Who are you?

Take a look at the following descriptions and select the one which is
most like you. I am...

1. Artistic, intellectual and/or non-conforming
2. Energetic, competitive and/or outdoorsy
3. Charismatic, alluring and/or fun-loving
4. Conservative, nurturing and/or a homemaker
5. Refined, organized and/or meticulous

If you chose 1, you are a Philosopher.

You like your clothes to be different. Your signature style is creative. Choose trends that reflect **Water** energetic design elements: dark colors, wavy patterns; fluid or sheer fabrics; velvety textures; flowing or asymmetrical shapes; unique styling.

If you chose 2, you are a Pioneer.

You like your clothes to be comfortable. Your signature style is sporty. Choose trends that reflect **Wood** energetic design elements: blues and greens, stripes or florals, natural fiber fabrics, columnar shapes, pants, casual or athletic styling.

If you chose 3, you are a Pleasure Seeker.

You like your clothes to attract attention. Your personal style is dramatic. Choose trends that reflect **Fire** energetic design elements: reds and purples, pointed or angular shapes, animal prints and fabrics, attention-getting or body-contouring styling.

If you chose 4, you are a Peacemaker.

You like to be conservative. Your personal style is traditional. Choose trends that reflect **Earth** energetic design elements: browns, yellows and earth tones; squared shapes; basic fabrics; nubby textures; comfortable or classic styling.

If you chose 5, you are a Perfectionist.

You like your clothes to be the best. Your personal style is elegant. Choose trends that reflect **Metal** energetic design elements: white, pastels or metallic; rounded or arched shapes; luxurious fabrics; polished textures; elegant or designer styling.

These represent your essence, or your core being, and each one uses one of nature's five elements—Water, Wood, Fire, Earth and Metal—to describe physical appearance, preferences and goals, lifestyle, and clothing design elements. By adding these elements to the way you dress, you will always be true to yourself and your essential being.

For me, indigo purple is a Fire element and I am fundamentally a Pleasure Seeker. I have come to understand why I loved it so much, and now I have carte blanche to wear it. I may not always wear it close to my face but I have shoes, handbags and suede gloves as part of my regular clothing ensemble, and I feel so alive when I wear them—who says handbags can't change your mood? The best workshop I ever ran was for 60 of my image colleagues—always the most difficult as they continually appraise what you're wearing! I wore a V-necked purple dress with matching purple pants with black pointed toe stilettos in patent leather. My Fire outfit enabled me to shine in the spotlight, have some fun and connect with my audience because I was allowing myself to be authentic.

Essential uniqueness

I stress the point here that my version of Fire will not be yours. I share my Fire essence with an almost equal amount of Wood and this certainly tells me why I'm never out of my jeans and am always doing stuff rather than just being. So, my Fire will be tempered by a need for speed and movement. Add into the mix my personal body shape, coloring and current intention (see below) and suddenly I've made this style my own. Mine—not anyone else's.

In order to look our best, our clothing should always suit our body shape, coloring, life style and personality, and this is fundamental. But what if we need to introduce a new element into our lives? If life is hectic, we need calm. If it's boring, we need excitement. What about the things we desire? To be more grounded, to have freedom, to have fun and so on. Applying the Fashion Feng Shui® principles can help us, even if it's something you desire for a very short time, such as being nurtured when you are feeling ill.

This is called **intentional dressing**.

Here is an overview of the basic principles and how you can use them to realize your "intention."

Water is introspective and indicates "being." If you want to attract more depth, quiet, stillness or tranquility, wear clothes in black or dark tones, in an asymmetric pattern such as paisley. Fabrics should be fluid, flowing, sheer or drapy. The overall effect is undulating and soft.

Wood is dynamic and indicates "doing." Clothes that support this should be blue or green, columnar in shape and pattern (including vertical stripes, ribbing, corduroy) or of a floral theme. Fabrics should be crisp or springy. Jeans fit into this category extremely well. The overall effect is vertical and active.

Fire is dramatic and indicates "exciting." To bring energy and radiance into your life, you will need to bring out red and purple. If you can't wear red in your clothing, think about introducing a red accessory such as a watch, handbag or shoes. Fire also embraces animal prints and diamond or triangular patterns in clingy fabrics or natural ones such as leather, fur, taffeta, wool or silk. The overall effect is angular and bold.

Earth is traditional and indicates "nurturing." If you need to be grounded, turn to earthy colors such as yellow and brown. Plaids, checks and boxy styles in coarse or nubby textures give the feeling of being cared for. The overall effect is boxy and square with horizontal lines in the garment.

Metal is elegant and indicates "refinement." It includes white, pastel and metallic colors. Luxurious, shimmering fabrics are the clothes to introduce if you want to attract more precision and polish. Arched or dotty patterns suit this well, too. The overall effect is figure-eight and curvy.

During a Fashion Feng Shui® consultation, you'll be given body color wands that reflect your hair, eye and skin tones. Elemental skin tones create a corporal connection and are ideal for underwear and footwear. Eye colors enhance interpersonal integrity and are best worn on the upper body. Hair color is worn as an outer garment or an investment garment and provides overall balance. As these shades are predominantly neutral, they are ideal for handbags, shoes, outerwear, skirts and trousers.

Use these guidelines in conjunction with what you know about your own style preferences and you'll soon see a difference. My own clients were skeptical at first, but once they had been through the consultation, they all agreed it was life-changing. The concept of aligning the physical body with the mind and spirit is what makes this so wonderful to work with. By applying these basic principles you can elevate what was once a mundane routine to a mindful ritual, so that getting dressed becomes easy, fun and empowering.

Take note of your Fashion Feng Shui® tendencies and try to incorporate them into your everyday life. If you need to take action at work, dress appropriately for your workplace and your body shape but add some Wood element and you'll be sure to get the work done.

Provenance and sustainability

The principles of Fashion Feng Shui® can be followed even further, specifically when you are purchasing clothes. Garments can retain the energy of their previous lives, so it is important to be aware of their vibrational quality and history, or provenance.

Clothes that are made from organically produced materials have more positive associations or happy memories attached to them. Clothes made by loving hands or socially responsible, environmentally friendly companies will have a corresponding beneficial impact on you. Those manufactured from tainted materials or in unpleasant surroundings may affect you negatively. Clothes, like food, are best when consumed as close as possible to their natural state. The less processing a garment has gone through, the fewer the opportunities it has had to pick up negative vibes along the way from its production to point-of-sale.

Why Fashion Feng Shui® is so important today

Let's look at the **corporate arena** first. In the past we spoke of the concept of first impressions. Having a professional dress code, looking good in a suit and having a personal brand were the ultimate goals. Unfortunately, this is not as "cut and dried" as it used to be. We can't make assumptions about clothing within the work environment anymore. Today, we need to talk about story, having screen presence, standing out and communicating from a distance. Leadership will now be about influence, warmth and trust as well as power and respect. Building strong, sustainable relationships has never been more important. This cannot be achieved unless your attire is authentic. It needs to represent who you are, what you stand for and your overriding goals at this point. Dressing to be someone other than yourself is called "acting." In the long term it can be exhausting and unsustainable. There is now a multitude of different ways to be successful in business. The main one is doing it your way. Fashion Feng Shui® will assist you to find that way.

The world is changing in our **day-to-day** lives too. The rise of social media means that we know what people in every country of the world are now wearing. Young people no longer listen to in-store sales consultants, but post "chelfies" (selfies taken in the changing room) to ask their friends if something suits them before they buy. Social media has presented us with the notion that we all need to have perfect bodies and perfect lives. Whatever your age, there is the underlying feeling that if you are not beautiful with a perfect body you have somehow "failed." Forget elasticated waistbands. The rise of older models, such as Dame Helen Mirren, means that you can't grow old gracefully anymore. But don't worry. Fashion Feng Shui® will **empower** you to be your very best, and most comfortable, self with your consultant as your guide, best friend, cheerleader. **When you find your own way, you own it.** What could be better than that?

Let me refer back to TV programs such as *What Not To Wear*, *How to Look Good Naked* and *10 Years Younger*. Most of the women (and men) on those shows were totally transformed. It's telling, however, that when a host went back 12 months later, most of the women on the show had reverted back to their original style. They had been **told what to wear,** and not been given the power to find out for themselves. They didn't own their transformation.

True transformation is more than just changing the way you dress. It's an alignment of who you are, what you love, what you want, how you live and how you translate that into your wardrobe. It's "your story." We call it the **transformation triad**. Representing the internal you on your external body so it's totally congruent wherever you are, who ever you're with, what ever you're doing and however you are feeling about life at any given time. One of my personal mantras is "Life evolves, style evolves." Fashion Feng Shui® enables you to evolve without losing sight of who you are. This means you move effortlessly with flow, balance and harmony into each period of your life.

Once you get used to this new way of dressing, you may even find that your intuition drives you towards what you need, energetically. A few years ago I was totally obsessed by burnt orange-colored clothing. I also craved foods with this color such as carrots, squash, sweet potatoes and most other root vegetables. As this color does not suit me on any level, I was quite surprised to find that it looked really good. It was also intriguing that sales assistants, and my husband, kept choosing it for me when I was shopping. On visiting my acupuncturist, I discovered that I had a depleted spleen. Basically, my batteries were flat. You guessed it. The spleen is an earth organ and I was wearing (and eating) burnt orange (an earth color) that could heal me. Powerful stuff!

I hope you find the following chapters in this book inspiring, illuminating and uplifting. The world is crying out for a more holistic approach to how we live our lives, how we do business, how we relate to other people and this includes how we dress. Our image is a HUGE part of ourselves. We all have to wear clothes, right?

See if you can make that part of your everyday routine as wonderful as the rest of you. Be guided by the other people in this book whose lives have been transformed for the better.

Just think of the possibilities and opportunities that are out there for you. By changing your clothes, the Fashion Feng Shui® way, they could become a reality!

Sue Donnelly
AICI CIP, FFSM, WYEF, LFIPI

Fashion Feng Shui® Master Facilitator,
Work Your Element™ Facilitator
and Lead Trainer
United Kingdom

Styling Your Soul, Spirit and Silhouette

+44 7984 153368
sue@suedonnelly.com
www.suedonnelly.com

Sue Donnelly worked within the travel and banking industries for many years before turning her attention to image. Despite always getting the best grades and exceeding workplace expectations she always seemed to miss out on promotions, failing to climb the corporate ladder. A session with an image consultant changed all of that. It was the first time Sue had realized the direct correlation between who you are, what you do and how you appear to others.

In 2004, Sue made the conscious decision to move into the image industry so she could help others gain confidence and self-esteem through their clothing choices. With a desire to be the very best she could be, Sue traveled the globe, learning from every expert she could find. However, it was only when she met Evana Maggiore, founder of Fashion Feng Shui®, that everything she had studied suddenly made sense.

Sue is now an international image professional of repute and the winner of the Association of Image Consultants International's Jane Segerstrom Award. She is a former president, a life member and an assessor of the Federation of Image Professionals International and a founding member of the Association of Stylists and Image Professionals. She is an AICI certified image professional and the Lead Trainer and the sole Fashion Feng Shui® Master in the UK. She is a licensed practitioner of Clarity4D and an NLP Level I practitioner.

Sue is a certified coach, a facilitator, the author of five books and a regular style expert in magazines and on TV. She has presented sessions on image-related topics all over the world. She believes that being authentically curious and allowing yourself to evolve are the keys to success— and that includes how you choose to adorn yourself and how you live your life, regardless of age, shape, size, background or lifestyle.

Her personal mantra: **one size does not fit all**!

Recognizing Your True Self with Fashion Feng Shui®

By Anita Marie Bangerter

"I saw her pass by, and I'll remember her until I die!" Has anyone ever made that kind of indelible impression on you in the fleeting moment of a glance? We all have the opportunity each and every day to "make an impression" on everyone around us. Why not make the most of this opportunity and use it to impact, to call attention, to attract, to influence or to promote. What a powerful tool we have at our fingertips, right before our eyes! Ourselves!

When you see someone "all put together," have you ever wondered how they do that? Perhaps you think to yourself they are so "naturally" talented, or they are so attractive, or they must have their own personal stylist! Do you self-sabotage the idea by telling yourself it's impossible to do that yourself, by creating stories that you can't compete? So not true! There is an order, a plan, a method, with tools that can be learned and applied, that actually work, for each and every person to "get it together." Each person's style or look can be "tailor-made" just for the individual, but how is this done?

It all starts on the inside. Now that's weird! What does the inside have to do with how someone looks on the outside? Simple! How you show up on the outside and present yourself to the world is a reflection of who you are at your core. This is referred to as your essence. It envelops every aspect of your innate nature. That means it is who you were from conception. It is what is stamped into your DNA. It is the whole package, your sex, size, shape, facial features, coloring, thoughts, beliefs, temperament, interests, gifts, voice, mannerisms, time and location of your birth, schooling and influences from others, genetics and family. It is your personal filter through which you view the world. Like snowflakes, everyone's filter is unique and different. Yes, you are

19

a one-of-a-kind, special, unique individual. Do you know who you are? Do you know yourself?

"To thine own self be true." What does that really mean? Explore this thought as you continue to be curious about yourself. Get to know yourself. Who do you think you are? Here is your opportunity, your invitation, to avail yourself of a special tool created to help you make your own self-discovery. This tool is called Fashion Feng Shui®. Take this quiz to get you thinking about who you truly are.

Read each question carefully and select the one response that best matches how you see yourself.

Which compliment resonates most with you?

1. You are a great resource to help me understand things I would miss on my own. You are so observant, wise and insightful, yet never intrusive or judgmental. You are a calming influence for me.
2. You always help me see the big picture and keep me focused on the goal. I get so much done because of you.
3. You make me happy. You are a breath of fresh air making any mood or situation lighter and brighter and full of renewed hope. You are always open and accepting and without judgment. Your enthusiasm for life is contagious.
4. You are a true friend and make me feel comfortable and accepted. You are always loyal, helpful and thoughtful. I know I can lean on you when I need to.
5. You have such a good eye for making everything look spectacular and classy. You inspire me to raise the bar to be more organized and to pay more attention to details.

Choose which place you might prefer to hang out.

1. Heaven on Earth for me is in a library or bookstore, walking on the beach or at an intimate jazz club.
2. I get my kicks hanging out at a gym or spa, in a park, on a bike or running trail or at a lively sports bar.
3. I love to be where there's action and fun—think resort, theater, amusement park, party or nightclub.
4. I am most comfortable at home with food, family and friends. I like a familiar place or activity, a community endeavor, volunteering, a homey restaurant or a garden center.
5. I love to dress up for fine dining or a special activity. I enjoy going to a museum, a live concert hall, a country club, a friend's beautiful home or on a planned dinner cruise.

What is important to you?

1. I treasure freedom, open space, alone time, thinking, independence, creative self-expression, relaxation, reserved and deep dialogue.
2. I am pragmatic, and I value logic, routine and plans, freedom to move, getting the task done, checklists, results, expansion, growth, competition, achievement, learning, adventure, direct dialogue, health and comfort.
3. It's important to me to have relationships that promote personal connection, socializing, play, fun, laughter, excitement, attention, open dialogue, options and variety.
4. I appreciate stability, security, support, peace, feeling needed, serving, consistency, helping others, tradition, being practical, follow-through and nurturing relationships.
5. My priority list includes these values: order, quality over quantity, excellence, control, respect, aesthetics, beauty and status.

An attribute you might struggle with:

1. Some issues I struggle with include feeling misunderstood or being left out, fear, close quarters, schedules and time restraints, rules, dress codes, noise, crowds and bright lights.
2. Sometimes I struggle with inner tension, headaches, tight muscles, anger, exhaustion or obsessive thoughts.
3. Sometimes I do or say something before I think and then feel bad. I can make hasty decisions or actions and later regret it. Some things I struggle with include not being taken seriously and feeling moody or vulnerable. I get bored easily.
4. I can feel strongly about something and appear stubborn, not open to change and stuck in old habits. I need to take better care of myself and not be so worried about everything and everyone. I need to learn how to say no.
5. I like things to be perfect, so I can be rigid, perfectionist, unrealistic and impractical.

How would your friends describe your personality?

1. Unique, creative, a deep thinker, intuitive, persistent, original, wise, spiritual, sensitive, creative, mysterious, sensual, a free spirit, a slow talker.
2. Competitive, physically active, determined, productive, self-disciplined, goal-driven, optimistic, confident, direct, assertive, ambitious, dynamic, a quick thinker, vocal.
3. Persuasive, openhearted, friendly, spontaneous, fun, inspiring, charismatic, vivacious, inspiring, a fast talker, passionate, empathetic, enthusiastic, impulsive, expressive, animated, dramatic, an attention seeker.
4. Committed, reliable, generous, service-oriented, kind and loving, dependable, conservative, sympathetic, helpful, diplomatic, grounded, responsible, nurturing, comforting, attentive.
5. Aware, gracious, visionary, perfectionist, orderly, demanding, cultured, refined, having good taste, detail-oriented, appropriate, meticulous, analytical, elegant, discerning.

What is your relationship with time?

1. I often loose track of time and am sometimes late to appointments. I am a night owl. I need time to process my thoughts. I go with the flow.
2. There is never enough time to do everything so I get up early and often stay up late to get the job done. There is always something to do, so I prefer to schedule my day and follow a routine. I can burn the candle at both ends.
3. I love to have a good time. I like to be open and flexible for the best opportunity that comes up and then decide what I want to do. I like free time to scan options and be spontaneous. I hate schedules!
4. I like to live in the moment. Time is irrelevant to whatever is needed outside of my regular set routine. I can drop everything if I am needed.
5. Time is precious, so I make plans ahead and schedule myself to make sure everything is covered. My planner helps me pace and track what I need to do without forgetting anything.

What does your day look like?

1. I start late and stay up late. I am slow, calm and stay away from distractions. I have a flow and alternate between doing and thinking.
2. I rise early and follow my routine quickly. I take action to get the job done. I am always talking, doing and moving toward a goal. I make and follow a plan.
3. I don't always know what I am going to do. I am open and receptive to respond to whatever comes up. I'm uninhibited, excitable, spontaneous, quick and reactive. I like variety.
4. I prefer routine and the familiar and convenient. I am content to sit and watch and be passive. This allows me to be available.
5. I prefer a predicable routine. This allows me to be ready, deliberate and proactive without surprises. My movement is precise, appropriate and organized.

Which group of words might you use to best describe yourself?

1. Intellectual, artistic, reflective, spiritual, mysterious, creative, non-conforming.
2. Energetic, action-oriented, motivating, casual, competitive, outdoorsy.
3. Charismatic, engaging, high-energy, alluring, fun-loving.
4. Pragmatic, traditional, dependable, practical, grounded, nurturing, a homebody.
5. Polite, appropriate, quality-driven with an eye for beauty and excellence, organized, meticulous.

Do you have any of these health concerns?

1. I have had or still have health concerns related to one or more of the following: kidney or bladder, reproductive organs, bones or teeth, thyroid, hormones, arthritis, circulation, hearing.
2. I have had or still have health concerns related to one or more of the following: liver or gall bladder, tendons or ligaments, headaches or migraines, joint problems, vision, depression, addiction.
3. I have had or still have health concerns related to one or more of the following: heart or small intestine, insomnia, panic attacks, inflammation, rashes, epilepsy, stuttering, attention span.
4. I have had or still have health concerns related to one or more of the following: stomach or spleen, eating, digestion, elimination, diabetes, weight, gums, lips, lethargy.
5. I have had or still have health concerns related to one or more of the following: lungs or large intestine, allergies, irritable bowel, autoimmune, sensitivity, flexibility and stiffness, compulsivity.

How do you remember your childhood?

1. As a child, I often played alone and had imaginary friends. I enjoyed anything creative or artsy. I kept a diary. I loved magic and mystery. I was social but quiet. I enjoyed taking art classes.

2. I was always reminded to be quiet and sit still. I loved anything physical like gymnastics, biking, skating or building blocks. I preferred outside activity. I was out to win any competition.

3. I had lots of friends and was a social butterfly. I enjoyed anything new, and was into trying everything because I got bored easily. I was really good at memory games. I am still a kid at heart.

4. I was a homebody and enjoyed family more than friends. I learned to cook at a young age. I helped plan and set up special gatherings. I had a cozy reading corner with many books. I liked to collect and display things. I still have some mementos from my childhood.

5. I liked to have my room very neat and organized. I decorated my room and picked out the colors. I enjoyed puzzles, painting by numbers, origami and putting things together. I liked my planner book.

When you look in the mirror, what body movements and mannerisms do you see?

1. I like to go at my own pace, which is slow. I am pensive and I think before speaking. My voice is low and slow and flows as I think. I prefer reclining.

2. I am a real Energizer Bunny™! I have a bounce to my step and my voice. My voice is bold, direct and fast, and I often speak in clipped phrases. I appear to be casual, with hands on hips, fists clenched and finger pointed, and my feet are planted solidly, equally apart. This keeps me ready to go.

3. I am a busy bee, always talking, scanning, and moving my hands and feet all the while. I even talk to myself! I get fidgety. I can easily get excited and demonstrative.

4. I am known as the mother hen and like to watch over my family and friends. This means I like to touch and hug people. I am usually relaxed and down-to-earth with open arms. I am open and receptive, and I like sitting in a comfy chair when possible.

5. I take pride in being composed and appropriate for the occasion in my appearance, voice and body. I have learned how to fold my hands and cross or not cross my legs (depending on the situation), keeping them held tight to my body. I am sensitive to not impose on another person's space. Good posture is important, as are good manners.

What best reflects your view of fitness?

1. If I were to exercise, it would be something that is free-flowing, like Tai Chi, Qigong, yoga, modern dance or perhaps ballroom dance. I enjoy the solitude of walking along the seashore by myself to think and breathe fresh air.

2. I enjoy disciplined exercise at a club, especially weight training. Even better would be an outdoor activity like rock climbing, wind surfing or mountain biking. I like to compete with myself to see how much better I can become.

3. I enjoy working out to lively music with a fun group of people. A dance class like Zumba® or salsa would be energizing and social. I like to do different things and not be on a rigid schedule to exercise the same way every day.

4. I don't love to exercise, so I am more successful if I commit to exercise with a friend or group to keep me motivated. I feel committed if I belong to a club or class or make a date with a friend.

5. Gyms can be grungy and gym-goers unsavory, and I might be self-conscious in a group class. Perhaps my best option is to get a home gym or workout plan, or perhaps find a personal trainer.

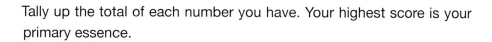

Tally up the total of each number you have. Your highest score is your primary essence.

1._____   2._____   3._____   4._____   5._____

1. **Water—The Philosopher**: intuitive, introspective, unique, goes with the flow, thinks out of the box, imaginative, creative, reflective, quiet.

2. **Wood—The Pioneer**: action-oriented, goal-driven, direct, decisive, logical.

3. **Fire—The Pleasure Seeker**: outgoing, friendly, emotionally aware, enthusiastic, positive, spontaneous, vibrant, social.

4. **Earth—The Peacemaker**: nurturing, grounded, reliable, stable, committed, compassionate, caring.

5. **Metal—The Perfectionist**: disciplined, organized, appropriate, discreet, with an eye for beauty and high standards.

You have now taken your first step to putting your personal puzzle together. Congratulations! Be patient with yourself as you get to know

and understand yourself better. If you were torn between two different archetypes, it could mean you have a strong influencing essence. Your primary and influencing essences are your personal portal to self- understanding. Keep them in mind as you make your way through this book and start recognizing your true self. Enjoy your journey!

Anita Marie Bangerter
MA, FFSF, WYEF

Fashion Feng Shui® Facilitator,
Work Your Element™ Facilitator, Life
Coach, Interior/Exterior Designer
Western United States

+1 801-910-4200
anitamarie328@gmail.com
gethertogether.com

Anita Bangerter is a woman of many talents and experiences. She is a mom, nana, educator, writer, speaker, designer, health and wellness coach, personal style coach, mentor, herbalist, photographer, master gardener, lover of nature, fitness freak, face reader, 9 Star Ki junkie, organizer and lifelong student—a true gatherer and disperser of information. She loves learning and sharing her wisdom and knowledge. She loves life.

The recipient of the Woman of Distinction Award in college, she went on to get a B.S. degree in Clothing & Textiles and a Master's Degree in Family & Consumer Sciences. She has taught high school, college (California Polytechnic) and community education adult classes. She has done interior design and space planning work in both the commercial and residential spheres.

Anita owned and operated her own home interior and gift shop called Apropos. Recently she has found the freedom to pursue current knowledge in areas she is passionate about, including certification as a health coach from the Institute of Integrative Nutrition in New York and certification in raw foods from Graff Academy and Tuscany Cooking School. She studied herbology with Angela Harris, face reading and 9 Star Ki with Jean Haner, body language with Kirk Duncan and energy work with LaRee Westover, as well as Feng Shui.

Anita is a longtime advocate and promoter of health and well being through alternative and natural whole foods and lifestyle choices. She strives to teach wholeness that includes aligning conscious awareness of the inside with the outside. She is available to teach whole well being and style coaching one-on-one and to groups. The content of what she teaches is individualized to meet the needs and interests of her client. Her passion is to teach clients to recognize themselves by discovering who they are on the inside and become who they aspire to be. Then she can help them develop a wardrobe that reflects their inner core essence and lifestyle on the outside. Her sensitivity and intuition, along with her broad academic background and firsthand experience, bring a unique offering to her clients to help them achieve their goals.

Anita resides in both Salt Lake City, Utah and Carlsbad, California. She is a naturalized U.S. citizen, widow, mother of eight children (four natural and four adopted) and nana to 10 grandchildren.

The Art of Becoming Who You Already Are Through Fashion Feng Shui®

By Else Gammelgaard Madsen

Imagine yourself in Tuscany in the early 1500s. You are standing behind artist Michelangelo. He, in turn, is standing in front of raw marble stone, holding a hammer and a chisel. The block you are looking at had been badly damaged by a prior artist, but Michelangelo has an almost mystic belief that the figure he will carve already exists, fully formed within the block of stone. By studying the raw marble, and examining the pattern, he can sense the figure and begin to transform the stone. In fact, he once said: "I saw the angel in the marble and carved until I set him free."

Four years of hard work later, Michelangelo liberated from this rocky prison his creation—the magnificent statue of David.

I totally love this story, being a huge believer that we all have the possibility to create our ideal life, to carve out our authentic self. Who we are is the product of our intention, our essence and what we believe and do. Consciously or unconsciously, we are always sculpting our future.

Without conscious direction, your authentic self is beyond your control. But the good news is that if you know which tools to use to shape your piece of marble, you will be able to transform your look and your life. You are already an inspired, talented artist who can shape your own life. When you are ready to discover who you are and who you want to be, start by looking for your own angel in the marble.

At the center of your being you have the answer: you know who you are and you know what you want. Becoming the person you want to be begins with exploring who that person is. So, are you ready?

Why is discovering who you are and who you want to be important?

When I was invited to write a chapter in this book, I had no concerns or doubts about which topic I wanted to share with you.

For me, it all began with a single question: Who are you? At an Insights Discovery accreditation in Aarhus, Denmark, I was asked to answer this question in quite a different way than I was used to. I was invited to put on my self-appreciation glasses, and without being humble, introduce myself by using a positive word in connection with my name. The word had to start with the same letter as my name, and it was important that the word also reflected what I really valued about myself. I have always been a very emphatic person, so the answer came easily. I wrote down "Emphatic Else."

The power of this exercise is that it has you focus on yourself, thinking about who you are in a positive way. Quite often the words you choose reveal values and preferences that represent the energy of your essence and your spirit.

> "In oneself lies the whole world, and if you know how to look and learn, then the door is there and the key is in your hand. Nobody on earth can give you either that key or the door to open except yourself."
>
> ~ *Jiddu Krishnamurti*

During my years of working in the field of coaching and image management, I have noticed how many people are struggling to find meaning and purpose in life and how discovering your authentic self can make a huge difference.

If you want to understand who you really are, it will require awareness, continuous reflection and introspection. My wish is for my story to help you understand the power of transformational coaching and transformational dressing. Moreover, I hope that becoming aware of dressing with intention leads you to find the door—and the key—to the real you.

At this point, I invite you to suspend any possible judgment of or skepticism toward the topic. Instead, be playful with the concepts presented, and see if you can find a way to practically apply them.

You can start right now by answering the same question I had to answer: Who are you?

Acknowledge the power of personality

Many people believe that a person's character and personality are largely established by the age of seven. In recent research, scientists have shown how personality traits remain with us throughout our lives. We remain fundamentally, recognizably the same person. This speaks to the importance of understanding our essence because this is something that follows us wherever we go, over time and across various contexts. Life events still influence our behaviors, yet we must acknowledge the power of personality, which helps us understand our future behavior as well.

When I was 10 years old, I wanted to be a nurse or an archaeologist. I liked to take care of people and offer help where needed. However, I was also very fascinated by archeology after having read a book about the discovery of the nearly intact tomb of the Egyptian pharaoh Tutankhamun. As you will see from my biography, I became neither. However, when looking at life through the lens of Fashion Feng Shui®, I can focus on my core values and innate traits. I can truly see what kinds of people, places, pastimes and clothes make me feel that I'm "in my element." This, in turn, creates an awareness of my authentic self and puts me in touch with which elemental archetype I must consult to dress who I am—inside and outside.

Sometimes in life, we build pictures in our mind about the future. Some of these things work out; many are assigned to the realm of childish dreams.

The next questions to ask are: What did you want to be when you were 10 years old? And how does this match who you are and what you do today?

The beginning of a life-changing experiment

I start my story in Vienna on November 1, 2008. This was my first day of training in Fashion Feng Shui®. The program was presented by founder Evana Maggiore, and Andrea Dupont assisted. As an image consultant, I was already very familiar with the concept of dressing my physical self. I knew all about the colors that complimented my hair, eyes and skin and which clothing silhouette best fitted my body shape. However, I was very excited and curious about the idea of learning a mindful approach to getting dressed as well as encouraging conscious clothing choices in my life and my image consultations.

The first assignment was to fill in a pre-consultation form and respond to the following points:
1. List any specific concerns or issues you would like to address.
2. If there was one thing you could change about your self/life, what would it be?

In 2008, I was running my own color and image business alongside my job as a team leader in a large international organization. I was very happy with this job, working only 25 hours a week for a good salary and alongside a lot of wonderful people, plus a loving family around me. My work-life balance was perfect. I had time and freedom to study new things, gaining new knowledge and inspiration.

However, I also felt a need to find a way to use all the newly acquired knowledge the best possible way. When people asked me what I was doing, I found it difficult to answer because so much was going on. The many years of studying had also resulted in getting no time to exercise, which had caused weight gain. I had forgotten to take good care of myself.

Hence, my answers to the aforementioned points were:
1. I want to find my best way of working, to find my real strengths and to make a difference in people's life.
2. To take care of myself and to put overall well being into my life.

As I learned, my answers were linked to intentions associated with the elements of Earth—the Peacemaker, and Wood—the Pioneer. Thinking back to my career dreams as a 10-year-old, I wanted to be a nurse, representing commitment, compassion, support and trust, and an archaeologist, representing adventure, action and achievements. I now realized that the Peacemaker was my true essence, as it deeply matched my core values and the spirit that I was born with. Yet there I was with a wardrobe full of Water, Metal and Fire elements, none of which matched my intentions or, for that matter, my essence.

"A good intention clothes itself with power."

~ Ralph Waldo Emerson

As an experienced coach, I am used to focusing on goals. Now I was noticing that my focus suddenly changed. I found it more effective to focus on my intentions. What's more, I realized that you do not simply identify your intentions and then forget them; you live them every single day.

Seeing the elemental archetypes as human character types made a huge difference for me. To fully understand the impact that the power of dressing with intention has had in my life, it is useful to look back at some peak moments I experienced since 2008. In doing so, I reflect on how I made use of what I call my creative mentors and role models— that is, the archetypes associated with each element.

- The Philosopher
- The Pioneer
- The Pleasure Seeker
- The Peacemaker
- The Perfectionist

Being aware of which archetype to consult to honor my intention, my essence and my appearance has been life-changing.

My peak moments

In the spring of 2009, while I was at the beautiful Copthorne Hotel in Gatwick, the Pioneer spurred change and action in my life. Early in the morning, my boss phoned. He told me that the company had to down-size, and this meant that people in my department would have to go. I was busy finishing my certification in coaching and development, and as we spoke, I was inspired by the idea to take action, to get out of my comfort zone and leave my job. We agreed, and in September of that year, I left my safe job of 16 years to take a leap into something new. With my new Pioneer intention in mind, I changed from wearing wavy patterns, fluid textures and dark colors to wearing the blues and greens of my palette and natural fiber fabrics. A pair of trousers also sneaked into my wardrobe. I felt a lot of new energy and was inspired to move forward and take action.

This gave me the opportunity to set my sights on new horizons. My next step was to become an Insights Discovery licensed practitioner, help-ing people understand how they prefer to think, work and behave. My

Insights Discovery personal profile gave me new insights indeed and confirmed for me that my true essence is that of the Peacemaker, with influences from the Pleasure Seeker. As a Peacemaker, my style has always been very traditional and classic. By adding elements from the Pleasure Seeker, such as red, purple, lifelike patterns and eye-catching details, I began dressing more dramatically traditional, and really felt that power of dressing who I am—inside and out.

Throughout the years, I have regularly consulted these elemental arche-types. The Pleasure Seeker has helped me to attract fame and enthusi-asm, and this has resulted in several awards and interesting job oppor-tunities. Now I am aware of my strengths and very close to finding my best way of working by honoring my essence in everything I do. I have noticed that I feel good and balanced when I wear all five elements. I do not buy many clothes, shoes or accessories, but when I buy, I follow this advice from Evana herself: "No should and no must, only love."

I invite you to remember the image of Michelangelo. Now begin carving. The ideal life has many layers, and it is often helpful to be aware of how the layers are all related to each other.

Consider the following:

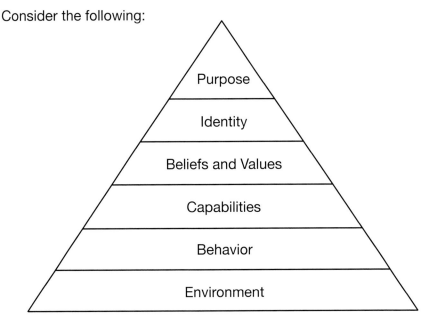

Based on the Neurological Levels concept developed by Robert Dilts (1990).

Imagine that you need to carve through these layers before you can release your angel. Making changes to a lower layer may, though does not necessarily have to, have an effect on an upper layer. However, an upper-layer change will have a distinct impact on the layer below it. Typically, a change is needed at a higher layer to enable success.

I began carving at the identity level. Where do you want to start?

Not sure? Just e-mail me, and I will send you a workbook for guidance.

Bridging the gap between present you and future you

Looking at the person I am now and the journey of my life since that November day in 2008 makes me realize how affected we all are by our environment at every moment, both consciously and less consciously. Often because of imposed requirements or guidelines, or because we have learned to tolerate or "make do" with less than ideal circumstances, we find ourselves in a work or a life environment that does not fully match the person we are or the person we want to be.

Knowing who you are and what you want to attract in your life is the key to learning how to make mindful choices. This is what makes the process of dressing with Fashion Feng Shui® so powerful. Buying items for the person you are now and for what your lifestyle is now will give you that feeling of fulfillment.

I sincerely hope that my story has inspired you to begin your journey by taking your first Fashion Feng Shui® steps. You, too, can bridge the gap between the present you and the future you by knowing who you are, doing what you love and being the person you always wanted to be.

Go experiment—have fun and happy exploring!

"We meet ourselves time and time again in a thousand disguises on the path to life."

~ *Carl Jung*

Else Gammelgaard Madsen
FFSM

Fashion Feng Shui® Master Facilitator,
Business and Image Management Coach
Denmark

*At the heart of my own values is
the importance of people.*

+45 50 50 24 58
info@full-circle-image.dk
www.full-circle-image.dk
www.nytimage.dk
www.imagemanagement.dk

Else Gammelgaard Madsen thrives on getting people to communicate more effectively and to understand themselves and others. She helps them tackle their most pressing challenges in business and life. Her passion lies in Fashion Feng Shui® and coaching and image management, where she is known for a holistic, positive and appreciative approach as well as her ability to inspire, excite and engage people.

Else founded her image management business in 1993. In 1994, she trained as a facilitator for Nyt Image, a Norwegian concept combining color, style, image, makeup, skincare and nail care with positive thinking and diet change. Else became Nyt Image's country manager and owner in Denmark, where she has trained 25 facilitators and helped thousands of women become more confident, positive, stylish, colorful and fit.

In 2006, seeking more knowledge in color and style techniques and wanting to bring her business to a new level, Else went to the UK to train with Style Directions. After four years of studies, she successfully completed the ICC International Coaching Certification Training and her education as a stress management consultant, an integration consultant and a licensed consultant for Insights Discovery in Denmark. She also trained as a facilitator in personal accountability with QBQ in the US and was awarded a Postgraduate Certificate in Coaching and Development at the University of Portsmouth in 2010. This led her to hold jobs as a facilitator, a coach, a manager, a leadership consultant, a mentor and an appointed external examiner in coaching, conflict management and general management.

During her studies, Else felt that something was missing. She found her shelf full of books about Feng Shui and one day the missing link became clear in a newsletter from Danish Feng Shui guru Ranvita La Cour. The newsletter mentioned Fashion Feng Shui® as something new and innovative. Else was inspired by what she read. By 2008, she was receiving training by Evana Maggiore in Vienna. In 2010, she became certified as Fashion Feng Shui® Master Facilitator for Scandinavia.

Besides Fashion Feng Shui®, Else specializes in professional image management, webinars and e-learning programs in color, style, positive thinking, diet change, solution-focused coaching and emotional intelligence. She holds motivational workshops in personal development, customer service, sales effectiveness, appreciative inquiry and personal accountability.

"But, Mom, This Is Me!"

What Can We Learn from Children About Authentic Personal Style?

By Andrea Dupont

> **"**Let the world know you as you are, not as you think you should be, because sooner or later—if you are posing, you will forget the pose, and then where are you?"
>
> *~ Fanny Brice*

There are many reasons why we look in our closet and think "I don't have a thing to wear." My own philosophy is based on a concept I have been researching for about ten years. The secret is in rediscovering who we are!

Just being yourself sounds simple enough, doesn't it? But is this the you that you're experiencing now, the one that your significant other knows, the one created by your parents' expectations and influenced by their peers? Or is it the one that you were born to be? The here and now is all we have, so let's start there and work backwards.

Do you remember how you were as a child?

Everyone is born exactly as they are meant to be. We come into this world with a personality trait, our own way of expressing ourselves. It has been established that from birth to about the age of five, we are encouraged to be as we are: cute, clever, smart, funny, creative, independent and determined. Nobody messes with who we are in these formative years.

Then we begin to be mainstreamed into society, we go to school and there the expectations start. We are expected to act a certain way, then there is bullying, competing, fitting in with the "popular" kids. We get pressure from our peers to be "cool," we are told by parents, guardians, teachers and friends, "Don't be so loud, sit still, don't speak unless spoken to, do better, be better."

As we know, kids can be especially cruel. Our confidence is tested at every turn, with negative messages that can cause self-doubt in many aspects of our lives. The things that stand out at an early age are the ones we carry around with us for a very long time; they impact our self-image and our sense of self in our relationships.

Children left to their own devices when expressing their personal style do much better later in life.

As crazy as it sounds, if children are allowed to express themselves at a young age through their clothing choices, it helps build self-confidence and encourages them to trust their instincts.

Clothes are an expression of our inner self, a way of showing up in the world. Were you allowed to make choices while growing up, were you free to choose your own clothing and the way you wore it, or did you need to conform to someone's idea of what was acceptable? Were you encouraged to express yourself verbally and through your clothing choices? What is the earliest memory you have of an item of clothing?

Do you remember if and when someone said something about your appearance that was a life-defining moment? Was it supportive or destructive? How old were you? Did someone ever say, "You're so pretty, if you only didn't have to wear glasses" Or did you have to wear hand-me-downs? Can you understand how this has affected how you see yourself as an adult?

Here's the story of an ugly duckling who was kissed by a frog at an early age.

As a child, I wasn't allowed to make my own choices, including about what I wore: most of my clothes were hand-me-downs, and I went to the parochial school, so, needless to say, I had very few choices to make (unless you count rolling up my skirt after I left the house).

When I was finally let loose in the stores with my first paycheck of $42.00, I was like a kid in a candy shop. This started my journey into the world of fashion: I was finally able to choose my own clothes. I tried them all! This had a huge impact on the choices I continued to make as an adult, regarding my clothes, relationships and bringing up my daughter.

If you identify with any of this, you can begin to understand the love-hate relationship we can have with our clothes. I got my messages from several sources, first and foremost from my French Catholic upbringing—need I say more? To some I don't have to explain, but basically the values instilled in me were to not stand out: "Don't be vain, think of others first, don't speak." I had no voice! It was all about what others would think or say. For a creative Water child like me, this was very difficult. It suppressed my uniqueness, my sense of freedom and the need to express myself, and impacted my self-confidence in many ways.

As parents, we mean well, and want our children to have the best and be the best. We don't set out to damage them, but we unwittingly impose our values and standards of what we learned on them, and so on and so on, for generations. I made a conscious effort to encourage my daughter to feel a sense of freedom, encouraging her to do her own thing, to express herself through her clothes.

It's important to let children have a voice, to allow them to have opinions, respectfully of course. Like most of us, I did repeat some learned behaviors from my upbringing. It's never too late to shift your perception and create a new perspective from which to see the world—your world as an adult or that of your child! We all have our own story about our childhood, and it's interesting to look at that and see how it has impacted the way we see the world through the eyes of our "inner child." That person is still there—your true self just got lost along the way.

The biggest lesson I learned from taking the Fashion Feng Shui® training was that it's not the clothes that should make you—you should be the one making the clothes. In order to do this, you need to know who you are. This is how my journey in discovering my authentic self began.

I had been posing, hiding behind a glittery facade. I thought this would help me fit in with the industry. I was showing up bold, I wanted people to see me as confident, as successful and as a person of great style, of course. I began to see that there was much more to looking good—it really wasn't just about the clothes. It takes courage to really look at yourself and ask, "Who am I?" But it's definitely worth it in the long run. The more I learned about who I was, the easier it became to express that on the outside. I stepped into my authentic self and everything else began to shift. I discovered my gift was showing my vulnerability, sharing my story. I was a visionary, and I saw "the possibilities."

In 2005, I became a grandmother. It's funny to see how milestones tend to impact us in so many different ways. My granddaughter was a gift that keeps giving back—she is my heart. She has always been encouraged to express herself verbally and, like her Mimi, in her eclectic tastes in clothes. She had her own thing going at an early age—she is a free spirit, a deep thinker who likes to be unique. My kind of girl! She is so much like me (that's her in the unmatched socks picture at the beginning of this chapter).

This is when I started to pay attention to other children and how they were expressing themselves by the outfits they wore. I began to see a pattern. I could also tell who was allowed to make their own choices and who was guided by parents or peers. It's amazing to see how they all were the visual story of how they saw themselves.

As a parent, we have a huge impact on our children's self-esteem, and encouraging them to be true to who they are is how it all begins. So here you are, a reflection of where you have been, feeling a sense of discontent. You know something isn't right, but you can't put your finger on it. I don't know who said this, but it's so true: "If you change the way you look at things, the things you look at will change."

Your physical self is always there; it's a visual message of who you are to the world. It's all about the choices we make, based on how we see the world, on our core values. It takes time and courage to really look at yourself and your life; we all come to that point at different times through different events in our life. Usually, a major life-changing event triggers the wish for something different for ourselves.

So how do we get there and how do we stay there? Why is Fashion Feng Shui® different and more impactful than traditional methods of discovering your own personal style?

It goes to the heart of who you are and helps you understand what that looks like, expressed in your clothes through color, shape and substance. It helps you stay in that place of knowing because it speaks to your authentic self. If you look back at your childhood, were you an independent free spirit? Were you an active tomboy with all sorts of plans? Were you a spitfire, digging in your heels, always ready for an adventure? Were you a child of habit and not a fan of change? Or were you meticulous and careful never to get dirty? As children, we want to please, so we conform to the expectations of our peers. The messages we receive at an early age, about how we behave and dress, stay with us and impact how we make choices late in life. Parents and peers in our formative years unknowingly pave the way for how we perceive ourselves when we become adults. Who we choose as friends and partners, what path we take professionally—they all bring us to a place that either fulfills us or causes us to question who we are. Clothing is one way for us to communicate with the world around us. Our clothes are our voice; they speak for us.

> "At the center of your being you have the answer: you know who you are and you know what you want."
>
> ~ *Lao Tsu*

I am giving you permission to step into your true self and grab what you want. It's a known fact that we cannot visualize what is not in us.

What is the one thing you would change if you could? The way you answer this question is very indicative of what isn't working in your life; we end where we began. Understand who and what you were brought into this world to be and do.

It's not too late to find your way back, or perhaps, most of all, help your children to maintain their innate personality and grow up more confident and self-aware. You can help them have a voice.

> "Because we have not taken the time to catch up with ourselves, we are living on the leftovers of where we have been or the preparation of where we are going."
>
> ~ *Debra Adele,* The Yamas and Neyamas

Andrea Dupont
FFSM, CECC, FSP

Fashion Feng Shui® Master Facilitator
Portsmouth, New Hampshire, USA

andrea@andreadupont.com
www.andreadupont.com

Andrea brings 25 years of experience into her holistic image and lifestyle consulting practice. She is passionate about helping people achieve all that they wish for in their life. By looking and living authentically, you are always aligned with what surrounds you. Andrea has designed and manufactured her own line of maternity clothes, owned and operated a women's specialty shop, and has been employed as a buyer and manager of several retail operations. She holds a degree in fashion merchandising and has extensive training in textiles, design, body image, behavioral science, the psychology of appearance, skin care, personality typing, face reading, color and figure analysis and Feng Shui.

Active in her community of Portsmouth, New Hampshire, Andrea is a professional image consultant, interior designer, color consultant, Feng Shui practitioner and Fashion Feng Shui® Master Facilitator. She offers live Fashion Feng Shui® facilitator trainings, workshops and individual consultations, Feng Shui lifestyle coaching, color consultations and Feng Shui space analysis. She is passionate about sharing her extensive knowledge and committed to making a difference in people's lives.

From Fear to Fortitude

How to Use Fashion Feng Shui® to Build Self-Confidence

By Dr. Carol Parker Walsh

"My self-esteem is high because I honor who I am."

~ Louise Hay

I was struck by several statistics I recently read around women's self-esteem, self-image and self-confidence. A simple Google search on "women self-esteem" yielded 42,800,000 results. "Women self-image" yielded 36,500,000 and "women self-confidence" gets 4,730,000. When I further narrowed my search to "midlife women body image," there were still 420,000 results. Even more staggering was a search for "teen girls self-image," which yielded 7,380,000.

These numbers clearly demonstrate that individuals are struggling to learn about, understand and embrace a positive and confident image of self. Even though my focus is on women, in this chapter men are not exempt from the conversation. There were over 30,404,000 search results for "men self-confidence".

As we're bombarded with so many conflicting messages on who and how we should be in the world, it's more important than ever to provide individuals with the tools they need to discover their authentic essence/self, and use this knowledge to move from fear and self-doubt to assuredness and confidence.

My relationship to this issue

Intersectionality was a concept I learned and studied in my doctoral program. Intersectionality studies the connection across various social identities, particularly those identities that have been subject to oppression and subjugation. Living along the margin at four of these intersections: gender, race, weight, and age, I was curious to understand how this played out and impacted my life and the life of others similarly situated.

When I sought to see myself at these intersections reflected in positive, uplifting, beautiful or even sensual ways, what I saw instead in the media was a litany of everything that was wrong with me. Age-defying makeup and skin care creams, weight loss tips and secrets, how-tos on changing your hair color and eye color, bleaching your skin, straightening your hair, curling your hair, etc. were the never-ending messages received on a constant basis. Upon further exploration I realized there was a high prevalence of body, image and age dissatisfaction among women at these intersections (as demonstrated by the Google searches).

The media communicates complex ideals around standards of beauty, which has served to shape the identity development of young girls and women. These often false and unrealistic images foster a negative self-perception of our bodies and self-image, which has a deleterious impact on our health, well-being and self-confidence. These unrealistic images and the constant push for perfection contribute significantly to eating disorders, obesity and high-blood pressure, and feed the cosmetic surgery industry in the billions. Dissatisfaction with one's body image leads to low self-esteem and a lack of self-confidence, and a lack of self-confidence can lead to depression. On average women are prone to comparison, often finding something wrong with themselves while finding perfection in others.

The explosion of social media has served to expand the idea of a singular image of beauty to include more and more marginalized women. Plus-size, advanced-age and culturally diverse women have rejected the media's idea of beauty and have allowed women of all ages and socioeconomic backgrounds to find supportive representatives of themselves. Despite the success of these communities giving voice and visibility to a broader population of women, they still fall short of supplying the necessary tools to adapt and change one's self-concept. This is where Fashion Feng Shui® comes to the rescue.

A new paradigm: Fashion Feng Shui®

A friend introduced me to the concept of using the principles of Feng Shui when building a wardrobe. I was intrigued by how Feng Shui asks deeper questions about who you are and how you show up in the world in order to gain an understanding of what to wear. Coupled with my previous research and recent certification as an image consultant, I pursued a certification and licensing in Fashion Feng Shui®. Although this now serves as the basis of my practice, the first application of this methodology was on me.

I've found that most people who have some success in life have done so through various trials and tribulations. I'm no different. I had a low point in my life when I lost a sense of myself, lost my confidence and lost who I was. Although ecstatic over being a mom to two beautiful children, I found myself in the process of going through a divorce. You may know what that feels like. I had gotten the hang of being a wife and a mother and owned those pieces of my identity, but somehow I forgot about myself along the way.

In addition, my body changed and became unrecognizable after having two children, and the weight I gained during those pregnancies unforgivingly clung to my body for several years to come. Needless to say, my wardrobe and sense of style were as lost as I was. I succumbed to a dark place, a place of fear and uncertainty. I felt undesirable and unworthy, and it definitely reflected in how I dressed. As the Jedi Master Yoda says, "Fear is the path to the dark side." Fear indeed clouds everything and is the path to poor self-esteem, self-image and self-confidence… the dark side.

What often gets overlooked in the process of and path to reclamation is your clothing. It's dismissed as irrelevant, trivial, or as possibly a by-product of the process. Clothing, fashion and style are seen as frivolous considerations for the superficial or self-involved. My friends, nothing could be further from the truth.

Clothing is one of the most intimate things you can engage with because it's one of the core necessities of life, right along with food and shelter. As such, it impacts every aspect and every area of our lives.

Through my own transformative Fashion Feng Shui® experience, I emerged spiritually, mentally and emotionally stronger, more self-assured and confident. I am the Philosopher. I embrace the Water energy and my deep-rooted value of freedom and independence. I threw out my frumpy functional clothes and replaced them with an eclectic array of pieces that support my essential need to explore and create. With my influencing essence of Fire, I built in fun, lively, engaging pieces in my wardrobe. And to reinforce my Wood intention to grow my business and attract attention, I added comfortable durable pieces. Once I owned the curvaceous nature of my body, I easily discovered pieces that flattered me and complemented the deep and mysterious tones of my natural body harmony colors.

Today I have a thriving business, I attract the clients I love and want to work with, and I have a new husband and a better relationship with my kiddos. I'm not just their mother, but also a woman they admire. This seemingly simple yet highly complex process of rediscovery empowered and changed my life. No longer living in fear and on the "dark side of the Force," I now attract fame and growth and inspire action.

The path to your authentic self

Psychologist William James described the basic duality of our perception of self to be composed of our thoughts and beliefs about ourselves—in other words, our self-concept. In Fashion Feng Shui®, this is known as the authentic self. Your authentic self is who you are before you changed your thoughts and beliefs about yourself because of external expectations, opinions or people. As we age, we often lose track of our authentic selves in lieu of a socially constructed view of ourselves. In fact, people spend very little time engaging in self-reflective or intro-spective work on the "who am I," unless they encounter something in the environment that causes some level of discomfort, dissonance or disconnect. Out of fear of not measuring up, not being liked, not being seen or not being accepted, we ignore those aspects of our authentic self and construct or take on a persona that is acceptable. Once the situation changes, we again adjust our persona. We do this on and on until we lose touch with the core of who we are.

Once we can rediscover and reclaim our authentic self through an examination of our internal standards, values and beliefs, we can begin to erode the fear of being our true selves. We can then develop a healthy self-esteem and confidently express who we are. We'll learn how to know, like and, most importantly trust ourselves.

Using the energetic language of nature's five elements, Water, Wood, Fire, Earth and Metal, you can begin to map out the path to self-con-fidence and a renewed sense of self. With this understanding you can dress your whole self to fulfill, fortify and flatter every aspect of you. Fashion Feng Shui® elevates what was once just a mundane routine to the mindful ritual of empowering affirmation.

As I moved into a stage of reclamation of my true and authentic self, I found that my essence was clearly the Philosopher, as I noted earlier. Initially, however, you would have been challenged to find my true essence because unconsciously I embraced an Earth Peacemaker persona. In retrospect, I believe my unconscious mind was seeking out comfort, stability and nurturing since I became a new mother, moved across the country and started the process of a divorce. The chaotic nature of my life needed something to ground me. As a new mother, my first thoughts were always "What's best for my kids?" As a result, I put myself last—always putting my children's needs above my own. In all honesty, I was living in fear, and the energy of the Peacemaker was a safe place for me to hide.

My wardrobe reflected the Earth energy with neutral colors, shapeless frocks and boxy, slightly oversized beige sweaters. Everything about my closet said practical, basic and uninspired. For some this would be a heavenly wardrobe, but for me, being a true Water, my clothing was mundane, unimaginative and ordinary. Needless to say, I was miserable. Living in an "energetic state" also diminished my ambition, my creativity, and prevented me from going after a career that would truly fulfill me.

Yes, the Peacemaker brought comfort and much needed security during this disruption in my life. But it was not my true essence. When you don't know your elemental essence, you can't truly know your authentic self. You run the risk of living as an alien in a foreign land. Without this understanding of self, you're susceptible to lower self-esteem, self-doubt, prone to blaming yourself for a variety of unrelated things, and at worst, having feelings of self-loathing.

Once I discovered my true authentic essence was the Philosopher, my life changed for the better. I first changed my wardrobe, adding in unique styles and patterns, deep rich colors and fluid flowing garments—things I'd always been attracted to but did not dare to wear. I felt empowered, confident and comfortable in my own skin. As my confidence increased, I left my job in academia and embarked upon the unpredictable life of an entrepreneur. Freedom and independence have always been two of my highest values, and I now embraced them fully. I'm often asked why, with a law degree, I don't practice law, or why, with a doctorate degree, I don't teach. My answer, in true Water form, is because I don't want to.

More accurately, the spiritual nature of the Water philosopher seeks to do deep, meaningful life-changing work. Today I work to give other women the freedom and independence that comes with the knowledge of self. I help them to live a mindful existence and use their clothing as a resource to reinforce self-confidence, self-love and self-worth.

Strategies to build self-confidence

Coming into the knowledge of self doesn't occur in an instant, but rather over gradual, gentle and incremental steps over time. In her book *Presence* (2015), Amy Cuddy talks about the little "nudges" we have to take consistently over time in order to create lasting change.

Once you understand where you're situated within the elemental energy, you can begin the process of effecting change and reinforcing self. Where do you begin this process? I've outlined three strategies that will help move you from fear to self-confidence.

1. Discover your passions

When we're very young, before we've been influenced by others opinions and experiences, we were in touch with our authentic selves.

You can learn a lot about your authentic self by exploring your past and rediscovering the things you felt passionate about. It could be ideas, possessions, activities, locations or people. Passion comes from deep within and it's a reflection of who you really are.

Passion Activity

1. Take a moment to describe anything you can remember about what you liked to do, what you liked to play with, your favorite season, time of day, vacation destination, how you played with others, or with whom you liked to spend your time. Relate these back to the five elemental energies and then find ways to engage in these things to reinforce your authentic self.

Passion Activity

2. Create a detailed visualization in your mind of yourself doing the things you love and engaging in your passion. Notice how your body responds and what feelings arise. Do you feel a rush of positive energy? Can you imagine yourself clearly? Now write down:

(a) what you are most passionate about;

(b) what that passion means to you; and

(c) which elemental energy your passion is most closely related to.

---

2. Mindset shift

Carol Dweck is a famous psychologist who talks about individuals having either a fixed mindset or a growth mindset. A fixed mindset has a limiting belief that prevents you from learning new things, adapting to change or believing in growth and achievement. As a result, such individuals rarely achieve things beyond the limited perception. A growth mindset is the exact opposite, and such individuals are life-long learners. In order to build self-confidence, you need to adapt a growth mindset.

Our mindset is the first step toward making something happen, and when we realize the power of our thoughts, we can use them to help create the life we want. Use the principles of Fashion Feng Shui® as the basis of your growth mindset. Reinforce the mindset you need to engage in behavioral activities to build that muscle.

Mindset Activity	
Element	**Action Steps**
Water	• Do something creative. • Reinforce your independence. • Take quiet moments throughout the day.
Wood	• Do something active (walk or take the stairs). • Create a plan to improve a personal process. • Start a new project.
Fire	• Arrange to have friends over or go to lunch with business colleagues. • Attend a new networking event. • Reconnect with a few friends.
Earth	• Check in on clients and offer them an additional service. • Plan a clothing drive for the homeless. • Start addressing your holiday cards.
Metal	• Organize your closet or office. • Pick up a new painting or flowers. • Schedule your blog posts for the month.

3. Dress your authentic self

The final behavioral change or "nudge" will come in your clothing and how you dress. Dressing in alignment with your authentic self will serve as an affirmation and encourage reinforcement of our authentic self.

It's like the Pygmalion effect, or what's called a "self-fulfilling prophecy." This means that if we believe we will build our self-confidence by dressing in a particular manner, our elemental dressing will bring about self-confident behaviors. Visualization and mindset coupled with dressing our energetic self, are the key behavioral actions to moving from fear to confidence.

Dress Activity

Element	Dress Style
Water	The Philosopher loves dark colors like black and navy, flowy fabrics, unique designs and deeply values their freedom.
Wood	Always on the go and active, the Pioneer likes all things to be easy, natural and comfortable. Blues and greens in natural fibers suit this archetype.
Fire	The Pleasure Seeker loves having a selection of patterns and fabrics and tends to gravitate toward red, purple, animal print, leather and fur.
Earth	The Peacemaker loves traditional patterns, textured fabrics and chunky sweaters in browns, mustard and cream.
Metal	Tailored, high-end, luxurious fabrications in pastels, neutrals and soft metallics appeal to the Perfectionist.

Summary

I help passion-fueled, ambitious women of influence rise to their next level of success by first taking hold of their authentic presence, confidence and appearance. I work with them to stop letting fear and self-doubt keep them from reaching unimaginable heights in their life and business.

With startling frequency my clients tell me, "You changed my life! You taught me everything I never knew I needed!" Through tears, laughter and relief, my clients develop a new and stronger sense of self and confidence that has resulted in job offers, promotions, significant increase in profits, improved presentation skills and so much more.

But it wasn't I who changed their lives—it was the process, the system. And it's available to anyone who has vision, a growth mindset and the willingness to dress in alignment with their authentic self.

How do you view yourself? How would you like to be viewed by others? What would you do if you weren't afraid? What would you do if you felt confident and self-assured? What could you achieve if you no longer felt like a "fraud," or had to convince others to see the genius inside of you?

What's holding you back? Isn't it time you walked in that space? Isn't it time you stop hiding and stop letting fear rule your life and diminish your self-confidence?

Even after implementing these suggestions, you may still feel a bit stuck at building your self-confidence. Don't be discouraged and don't allow your frustrations to defeat you. You are victorious, and you can do this! I want to help you make this shift in order for you to be your very best, so that you can achieve the very best in your life and business. It's your turn, it's your time!

Dr. Carol Parker Walsh
JD, PhD, FFSM, AICI CIC

Fashion Feng Shui® Master Facilitator,
Work Your Element™ Facilitator
United States

Evolve Image Consulting, LCC
*Transform your life and business
through your wardrobe*

+1 360 606 9595
carol@evolvingyourimage.com
www.evolvingyourimage.com

Dr. Carol Parker Walsh has been a successful executive and entrepreneur for over 25 years. After an extensive career as a labor and employment attorney in Chicago, Illinois and Portland, Oregon, Carol became a management and organizational consultant with Oregon Health & Science University, the largest employer in Portland. Quickly noticed for her work and business acumen, Carol became the associate director of professional and diversity development at one of the top nursing schools in the nation. Soon after, Carol became an award-winning assistant professor and founder of the school's Public Health program. After a year she became director of the Oregon Public Health program, overseeing faculty and students at Oregon State University, Portland State University, and Oregon Health & Science University. After completing post-graduate work in leadership and management development at Harvard University, Carol went on to become an associate professor, an associate dean and director of a graduate university in Santa Barbara, California.

Carol began her entrepreneurial career in 2009 with the launch of ParkerWalsh Consulting, a six-figure coaching, organizational and diversity development firm, which earned her a Woman of Achievement Iris Award. She was one of the top 1 percent of business developers in a direct sales jewelry company, where she built a sales force of 100+ women, promoted several leaders, and received numerous national awards including the #1 award out of 25,000+ for developing the fastest-growing team in the company.

Wanting to work more intimately with women on developing their professional presence, Carol shifted her focus and started Evolve Image Consulting, a professional and personal development company that educates high-achieving women on developing an effective, empowering and confident image. She is a licensed Fashion Feng Shui® Master Facilitator, an Association of Image Consultants International certified Image Consultant and a Certified Master NLP Practitioner. She holds a JD and a PhD, and combines her education and extensive experience to help her clients implement strategies to increase profit, productivity, self-confidence and success. She recently received the AICI SFBA Rising Star Award and was the People's Choice 2016 Best Wardrobe Stylist with the Portland Fashion & Style Awards.

Carol is a two-time Amazon best-selling author, writer, image coach and internationally sought speaker and television personality. Carol currently serves as president of the AICI San Francisco Bay Area Chapter, editor-in-chief of the *AICI Global* magazine, a monthly columnist writing "Dress Code" for the *Vancouver Business Journal* and the local style expert for *The Oregonian*. She appears monthly on KATU2's AM Northwest. She has been seen in The Huffington Post and on ABC, CBS, NBC and FOX.

Pick up Carol's #1 Amazon best-selling books *The Second Act* and *Your Clothes Speak!*

Go to http://carolparkerwalsh.me/, or contact Carol for a personal strategy session at http://bit.ly/VisualImpactSS.

Healing Yourself with Fashion Feng Shui®

By Stefania Rolandelli

> **"**If you are not comfortable in your own skin, you won't be comfortable in your own clothes."
>
> ~ *Iris Apfel*

It's inevitable: some mornings you waste hours completely lost in and consumed by your clothes because nothing is working. All that you possess is somehow too tight, too coarse, too short, too long, too big... Those are the mornings you are extremely harsh with yourself. Even if you hold your breath and stand on tiptoe, how you see yourself does not improve. Those are the mornings you allow yourself only a cursory glance in the mirror, then you immediately climb on the scale. Suddenly, a seemingly ordinary day gets built around an image that you do not recognize and dictated by a number that may reflect your bodyweight but, more than anything else, weighs on your self-esteem.

It's late, there's not much time left to get ready and you end up wearing your usual uniform. After all, it's a safe cover-up and lets you get away with not having to commit to yourself. Then you authorize yourself to seek refuge in all those gestures that have become so routine: absent-mindedly you grab something to fill your stomach, you cancel your gym session. You essentially stow away your planner full of dreams and intentions in a drawer, putting off until tomorrow all the promises you made yourself yesterday.

I know you need courage to say "Yes" to your life, to your authenticity, to your beauty, to your freedom, to your passions, to your emotions. When you do it, you make space for yourself. You realize that even on those mornings when you have tried to tame the clothing lions in the circus rings and ogled at the numbers on the scale like it was a freak show, YOU in fact have always been the same you!

When you can realize this, you make room for magic, the magic harmony between mind, body and soul. And when you are in harmony, every-thing falls into its right place in your life, in your closet, in your fridge and in the mirror. You stop procrastinating until tomorrow, and you feel the need to start right now: start a diet, go to the gym, take a break, work on your projects, realize your intentions, live your ideal life.

This is the exact same story my clients tell me. They always wait for that perfect day (usually it is a Monday) to respond, to do something good for themselves. The excuse is almost always that "there's no time." However, the worst is when they say that they have no time to waste.

Their days are always hectic, full of activities, providing a justification for not taking care of themselves. I remind them of the real meaning of practicing self-care.

- Self-care is not just making plans, but taking action.
- "Self" does not imply being selfish, but rather respecting oneself.
- Care is the most important act of survival.

I myself know how they feel when they fight themselves, when they look in the mirror, when they feel lost among the expectations to accomplish, when they suppress their desires and dreams due to lack of self-confidence, when their skin burns beneath their clothes and upon their soul.

There's a real adventure to starting all over again. It does not matter where you decide to start: color, texture, hairstyle, make-up, home or job. You have to feel it on your skin because your skin never lies.

This is exactly what my clients experience when they fully identify with their essence and heal themselves. They find their harmony. They feel colors and fabrics on their skin and they are curious to try and

experiment. They explore with their senses—seeing, feeling, touching, smelling, hearing. Plus, they learn how important it is to attach a feeling or an emotion to every single gesture and discovery because they form the map of their skin this way—this is how they design their authentic self. They succeed in feeling all the shades of their intimate identity and the interactions among them. They are able to create a balance between their inner self and their outer self and they get rid of any conditioning.

Even if they start with a small change, everybody around them immediately notices that there is something different, and it has nothing to do with their clothes, but with the energy that surrounds their skin, their aura. There is an energy that lights up their smile, their joy and their serenity. It's a healing process that comes from inside out and makes them self-confident. When my clients feel this, they know they are doing better and therefore are open to being admired and appreciated. But when this happens, they need to go even further and deeper in the healing process. They need to:

- Enhance their inner essence, honoring who they are; and
- Enhance their image by respecting their choices in clothes, diet and exercise.

This optimistic energy affects their whole life. It affects their professional attitude and permeates into their family circle. They succeed in completing projects they had once started but gave up. They succeed in bringing closure to scenarios that once hurt them. They know the healing process lies in self-discovery and that self-esteem influences image, but it runs much deeper than that. When they step out of their old roles, they lose that familiar protective layer of their second skin. Then, they discover who they really are, who they want to be and how to dress to be true to their essence.

It's not some superficial or merely aesthetic process. This involves personal feelings and a deep connection with identity, memory, sensuality and a conscious living skin. My clients learn to inhabit their own skin. They learn to respect who they are.

So you are wondering what the magic formula is, right? Well, the truth is that there is no magic formula. Rather, your answers can be found in Fashion Feng Shui®. This program helps you define your essence beyond fashion, trends, uniforms and schemes. You are the

sacred place where everything starts. You are the heart, setting the rhythm and the style of your journey. You have no rules to adhere to. Just let yourself be free to see, to speak, to feel your personal beauty. Respect your own and intimate truth, what burns inside and gives you the courage to say "no" to whatever does not resonate with you.

Case study: Cristiana

I have had the great pleasure to work with Cristiana. Having recovered from a long struggle with anorexia and bulimia, she had regained possession of her life, but needed to discover who she was at her core.

During our first session, on introducing the five elemental archetypes to her, I sensed that she was having great difficulties because she was both attracted to and frightened by them. I immediately understood that she needed more time to think about the personality descriptions, to feel inside which of the five most naturally resonated with her. We agreed that in one week's time, we would meet again.

Seven days later, she turned up with a shy smile. She knew who she was and had even created a diary full of images and words that supported her vision. Her essence was Water. She was eager to fully embrace this, but she was hesitant because she had to let go of all those past roles she was used to and even felt safe playing as a way to be accepted.

Being Water, she had to reflect on and find her own answers. That happened in her soul, that place where she could be alone in silence.

We took a look at her wardrobe and it was clear that she was stuck in limbo. There were:

- Jeans, stripes, floral prints: these gave her dynamism though in ways that encouraged moving away from her real being.
- Earth tones, checked prints, nubby textures: these committed her to roles oriented to others and thus completely forgetting her real being.
- Rounded shapes, pastel colors, elegant styling: these made her seem perfect in all she did though strictly limited her real being.

Unsurprisingly, she did not have anything in red, with pointed shapes or body-contouring. She loved to be alone, yes; but, above all, she did not know how to connect with others.

Oh yes, there was black in her closet, but she was trying to get rid of it because her family and friends convinced her that she had to stop hiding herself behind that "non-color."

There was so much confusion inside and even outside her that she had to rid her life of strategies and rules. Clarity had to come from her skin. It had everything to do with her senses, with the truth and the beauty she had inside. She did not need to hear anything that referenced the body, nothing about numbers, shapes or anything that would make her feel obliged to fit in!

It was my task to give her food for thought, but I could only do so through my open questions.

- If she wanted to express a positive emotion, what would she wear, and why?
- What was the piece of clothing that made her feel vulnerable, and why?
- What was her biggest dream when she dressed up/opened her closet?
- When did she feel she was her best self? At that moment, what was she doing? Who was she with? What was she wearing?
- What did she like to be noticed for?
- How did she feel when she was wearing something that irritated her skin and consequently, her soul?

Thanks to these questions and her own deep reflections, she understood that if she did not feel comfortable in her own skin, she could not feel comfortable in the world, no matter what she wore.

Having an essence of Water, Cristiana needed to establish a deep connection between her soul, her body and her mind. Yet, she was conscious that she also needed to find a balance with the other four essences that somehow were part of her life.

So she literally emptied her closet. Then she reorganized it according to her new unique and creative vision. Black and dark colors and unusual designs were stored up front. All the rest had to be versatile enough to be combined, as needed, with whatever else she wanted to wear to invite some different energy.

Christiana did the same in her life. She found a balance in her athletic activity by splitting sessions between yoga classes and water exercises.

She found a balance in her diet by learning to listen to her body. She decided not to say "no" to her social life, thus reconnecting with all her friends, now that she felt free to be who she was.

She could do all this because she was tenacious, intuitive and mainly because she did not have to follow any rules or methods. She just had to follow her own personal unique flow.

If you, too, are Water, you need time to live your emotions while undergoing your transformation. You need to make mistakes. You need to respect your hesitations. And you should avoid making any comparisons.

You naturally possess an inner knowing: you just have to trust your intuition and then benefit from your own ability to self-heal.

Case Study: Maura

Maura, whose essence was Wood, was so overwhelmed by her influencing Earth essence that she had completely lost her capacity for "doing." She was so committed to helping and supporting others that all her enthusiasm and optimism were dried up. She needed to move on without too much pondering!

We prepared an action plan together, which included fixing dates, tasks and goals. The plan was mandatory because she could do something with it and that kept her mentally busy. The plan was to:
- Study the design elements that she really liked;
- Reorganize her closet before our consultation;
- Surf the web for brands, styles and trends; and
- Start a diet and do regular exercise.

My biggest and hardest task was to keep her motivated, but thanks to short-term projects, she could see the results and was eager for the "what's next."

If you, too, are Wood, your healing process is part of your personal growth. You set your goal and you think, do and try — without hesitation or doubt –until you have reached it. You derive energy and motivation from your essence. Your skin is not some boundary or a limitation on you, but

rather offers a project you are interested in working on every single day. You need to feel comfortable in your skin, in your vision.

Case study: Alessandra

Alessandra, whose essence was Fire, was struggling tremendously with both Metal and Water energies and thus losing her innate joy. She was hiding and constraining her free spirit and her natural love for variety. She needed to step out of the shadow, shine in her light and ignite the passion that connected her with the world.

She wanted to have fun and be in the spotlight and this is how it worked for us: my sitting in silence, her chatting quickly. She needed to touch, to look at things, to play and to share her excitement with somebody. For my part, I had to keep her exuberance focused. I did this by posting simple, direct "what if" questions, the only ones that could help me help her reveal her big vision.

If you, too, are Fire and needing to heal yourself, you must feel the fun. You need to enjoy the process and you need to share it with somebody because to you, life is being the center of attention. You feel most at home when you are among people and your radiance embraces them. Your energy is fueled by your social life and by your love of life.

You know you have reached your goal when everybody around you notices you, your charisma and your light. You are an emotional being, and emotions play a great role in your impulsiveness. Your impulsiveness is what makes you feel comfortable in your own skin.

If your essence is Earth, you need to commit to yourself. You must treat yourself as you do those who are part of your life. You must be your first priority. You must reconnect with your own genuine desires. You need harmony within yourself, as you find answers in your family and their traditions. You are at ease when cooking, when sitting at the table and sipping a favorite cup of tea: this is the most comfortable cuddle you can have. It fuels your energy because you are nurturing yourself.

You feel responsible for your healing process and you must learn to help yourself, using your nurturing energy to strengthen yourself. Practicality is your comfort zone; you are being true to your skin when you are serene, grounded and safe. This is why you need simplicity, routines and a sense of timelessness. You need to build things to last; your sense of home is what most resonates with you because it keeps you focused on security.

If your essence is Metal, you feel the need to organize and control your healing process perfectly. You need to plan and be ready for any inconvenience it may cause. You will live by its rules so you know that you are doing the right thing. You need to keep your mind at work and train your eyes to pay attention to details and quality.

Meanwhile, you feed your own energy with grace and with good taste. You strive for beauty and excellence in whatever you do, whatever you buy and whatever you choose, including the words you speak.

You feel comfortable in your own skin when you feel perfectly orderly and put-together. This feeling emanates purity, both spiritually and materially. This is your aesthetic sense, which goes far beyond skin-deep, reaching into your core. Your harmony is the innate balance of your natural elegance with your minimalism and your simplicity, no matter how cultivated and refined you also come across.

Now it's your turn: unlock the drawer and take out your planner!

All the intentions and all the dreams you have sheltered there are your true healing power because they are the expression of your best self in your ideal life. They are your authentic self-statement.

Let's make this real. Start visualizing your new skin. Take out a white sheet of paper and fill it up with whatever lines or colors you want, or maybe with words or images. This should be a portrait of your own personal authentic story. You should see yourself in this new skin and give it a name, reflecting all the facets of all of you. Exclude nothing.

From skin to style: it's all about self-expression, knowing who you are and letting go!

Stefania Rolandelli

FFSF, WYEF

Fashion Feng Shui® Facilitator,
Work Your Element™ Facilitator
Bologna, Italy

Quintessenze
*Wear your emotions: the perfect suit does
not fit only your body, but also your soul*

+39 347 28 22 565
stefania@quintessenze.com
www.quintessenze.com

Stefania Rolandelli was born in Italy. She studied foreign languages and has traveled around the world for work. She has held many sales positions, learning on the job how to deal with men and women of all ages, nationalities, cultures and personalities.

She is a Fashion Feng Shui® Facilitator, a Work Your Element™ Facilitator and a coach.

Stefania loves to call herself a "style alchemist" because she does not tell you what you have to wear: her work consists of helping you put into practice a deep transformation that is visible in your appearance. She does not work your change: you do it with her and only after you have understood who you want to be. So when you look at yourself in the mirror, you can honestly declare, "Here I am, that is really me!"

Stefania herself once forgot how to truly look at herself. She understood that she had to allow herself to set out on a journey of rebirth, with the intention of finding real harmony in her core essence, her body and the world all around her. Now that she has succeeded in achieving that alignment, she is aware of it and knows that everybody else can also perceive it. She decided to explore the world of appearance and image because of its expressive strength and strong expressiveness. Her mantra is: "I want to look beyond what I see in order not to judge, but to attach a meaning to it."

Thanks to Fashion Feng Shui®, Stefania has even transformed her business, re-branding it from Origami to Quintessenze. She respects Fashion Feng Shui® because it embraces both the essence of, and the freedom to play with, colors, fabrics, lines, accessories and outfit combinations. The purpose is always to create a harmony of contrasts that permits thousands of shades of colors and exceptions to patterns—there are as many as there are each of us, for we are each unique and special.

Fashion Feng Shui® helps you define yourself, separate from fashion, trends, uniforms and other conventions. It helps you fulfill both your personal and professional intentions, not a moment too soon.

From Dreams to Reality
Creating Deliberate Intentions
Through Fashion Feng Shui®

By Beverley Eve Cole

We all have dreams, ambitions and hopes, then one day we find that we have left it to too late to realize them. We sometimes think or say, "I haven't got the time," or "I can't afford it, I'll get to it later," etc.

What happens is that we have unconsciously blocked our progress by setting up negative intentions that stop us from reaching those hopes and dreams. So, how do we make it easier to manifest our intentions?

Accentuating the positive
Let me give you some examples of positive intentions in my life.

When I was 16 years old, my mother and I returned to our home town of Liverpool after living in Canada for several years. I was very dissatisfied with this move and declared to my mother that I was not going to continue to live in England, and that I would immigrate to another country when I was old enough to be self-supporting. This was a big decision at a young age! I had set the intention but at that time had no idea how it was going to happen.

When I was 19, I met someone through my work who talked about an opportunity provided by the New Zealand government for a paid fare, accommodation and job in New Zealand. I realized this was the answer to my dream. I took the opportunity and have lived here ever since. This was a life-changing intention.

As years went by, I realized that if you really desire something enough, you see opportunities and take advantage of them.

I have manifested many things, including innovative business ventures, travel to interesting places, a successful career, a wonderful home and fulfilling relationships.

Since learning about conscious intention and how to use the principles of Fashion Feng Shui®, dressing with intention, I have had further successes.

For instance, while operating my last business, Fashion Academy (NZ) Ltd., which is a color and image consultant training school and supplier of image materials, I felt that there was a gap in the way the program was delivered. But when I looked at Evana Maggiore's program, Fashion Feng Shui®, I realized that it was the missing piece in the jigsaw, enabling people to recognize who and what they were, so that their personal style resonated with their authentic self.

Intention to effect change

I decided to have Evana train me as the first Fashion Feng Shui® Master Facilitator, so I would be able to train others in Australia and New Zealand to be facilitators.

To make this happen, and after reading Evana's book *Fashion Feng Shui: The Power of Dressing with Intention*, I made some changes to my wardrobe, favoring elegantly creative Water/Metal clothing over the Earth/Metal business suits that I had previously worn.

Against all odds, I journeyed from New Zealand to Boston, Massachusetts to attend a Fashion Feng Shui® facilitator training, which then led to my appointment as a master facilitator.

This was life-changing for myself and others.

I worked with the Fashion Feng Shui® concepts, creating a conscious intention by using clothing that resonated with me and fulfilled my desire to define and create who I wanted to be, my ideal self and lifestyle.

I organized my clothing wardrobe according to my essence, Water/Metal, which gave me elegantly creative styles to fulfill my spirit. And I decided to use the intention of Wood for motivation, spurring me to spread the word of Fashion Feng Shui® in Australasia.

I soon found that lots of creative ideas and projects started to flow into my mind, and I found it easy to put them into action, using my business networks to gain consultations and train facilitators.

After 25 years of directing my company, I decided to sell Fashion Academy (NZ) Ltd. so that I could devote more time to the more creative side of image consulting, including Fashion Feng Shui®.

I was unsure how to market the business to sell it, so I set my intention by using the Wood element in my clothing. This would help me to initiate change. I incorporated the colors green and blue, floral-printed scarves, hooded jackets, slim pants, etc.

Soon, people showed up in my life who were able to give me positive advice, and I was able to select the right buyer to carry on the business. My accountant was astounded at how quickly and easily the business was sold. Six years later, it is still thriving.

Another intention manifested when Evana Maggiore passed away. The business was then headed up by Andrew Maggiore, her son, who was looking for three facilitators to carry on the delivery of Fashion Feng Shui® virtual training. Even though I had never trained anyone virtually before, I decided that I would be one of the three, so I used the Metal element for focused action and became familiar with the online process. I was selected as one of the trainers—this has led me to carry out other virtual training and consultations for my color and image work, reaching clients and colleagues worldwide.

I would now like to present some case studies which illustrate some of the positive outcomes that my clients have achieved by using the principles of Fashion Feng Shui®.

Case study: Jude

Jude had set up a home-staging business to help people sell their homes. It was not going very well as she was an unknown in this field.

Jude is a warm, fun person who is passionate about her business and life. The Fire element resonated with her, tending to be sociable, expressive, warm and passionate.

She started wearing more dramatic styles using the color red, animal print scarves, leather jackets, etc. This got her noticed and allowed time to communicate enthusiastically with her prospective clients.

She applied elemental Wood as her intention for expansion and growth. Into her style, she added slim pants and sheath dresses in column or rectangle shapes reminiscent of the Wood element. She also included the color green, jersey-knit wool and floral prints.

Jude became more confident, wearing her personal styles and colors, and her business and personal lives improved enormously. Today she has so much business that she has taken on staff to assist her.

Case study: Sue

Sue is an accountant who works from home. She wanted a meaningful and fun relationship with a man. Her essence was Fire—passionate, charismatic, outgoing and full of fun.

The personal style that resonated with her, as an enthusiastic Fire soul, includes eye-catching details, silks, satins, real or fake furs, figure-hugging garments, deep V-neck tops, cashmere and leather pants.

To attract a committed partner into her life, she added some Earth elements, including structured garments, zippered jackets, brown pants, a leather square-shaped bag and square-shaped jewelry.

Today, she has a long-term partner, and together they share their hopes and dreams.

Case study: Jean

Jean came for a Fashion Feng Shui® consultation, and then decided to train to become a consultant. Her thinking was that she needed a career after her two sons left the nest. Her essence was Earth, the committed caregiver who is comfortable wearing classic traditional styles with simple interchangeable pieces, fabrics of soft textured wool, raw silk, vests, blazers and A-line skirts.

One of her dreams was to visit Italy, so we added some Wood elements to stimulate action for new horizons and travel. These included textured cottons, box-shaped wooded jewelry, ceramic beads, blues and greens in nubby fabrics, straight shifts with elongated, columnar lines and striped designs.

This gave her a comfortable sporty, traditional look that resonated with how she wanted to express herself. She soon realized that she preferred being a homemaker over having a career. A year later, Jean's husband was asked to attend a conference in Italy. She went along with him, making her dream come true by having dressed with intention.

My own story

I would like to share with you how I express Fashion Feng Shui® in my personal style.

My core elemental comfort zone fits with the elements of Water and Metal (elegantly creative styles). I tend to shop in upmarket boutique stores that carry unique, high-quality flowing styles.

As a Water person, I like to be an individual in my taste of clothing accessories, pastimes and home environment. You will find me traveling to places such as Morocco, Turkey, Italy and Spain.

My home is a mid-century modern house in the style of Frank Lloyd Wright and Richard Neutra. It sits on a ridge overlooking the water on eight acres of subtropical forest. I have furnished it with items that we have collected over the years; each has special significance and put all together, we have created our own eclectic style. There are Middle-Eastern rugs, batiks, offbeat colors, handmade furniture, antiques, paintings, books, etc.

My hobbies are reading, music, painting, watching documentaries, interior decorating, and healthy living. You will find me at art galleries, plays, festival films, libraries, upscale restaurants and funky cafes. Can you see why Water and Metal resonate with me?

Putting it together

My elegantly creative style expresses itself in choosing deep-to-medium muted colors and semi-fitted tops for the figure-eight body type. These choices correspond to the Metal body and Wood coloring, as I have ash-colored hair and green eyes.

I use unique, softly flowing, undulating semi-fitted styles with light- to medium-light fabrics and textures. My patterns are marked by paisley prints, waves and ethnic touches (Water). I go for polka dots (Metal) in scarves, pouch-shaped bags and round-toed shoes (Metal).

My costume jewelry is usually unique (Water) and of high quality, featuring gemstones (Metal). These styles appeal to my comfort zone yet support me spiritually, socially and environmentally.

The road between thought and expression brings me to the elements, which I add to my personal style when I want to manifest an intention. If the intention were to introduce more action and innovation in my life (Wood), I could add artistic floral designs, a unique-looking dark straw hat or bag, green colors, slim pants, a hood or a soft cotton scarf to my outfits.

If the intention were to have more fun, connect with people, get recognition, etc., I would incorporate some Fire designs. These could include a flowing red or purple scarf, uniquely dramatic jewelry, angular designs like a V-neck, a sheep skin jacket, a fur collar, a merino wool top, a silk scarf, and leather my shoes, belt or bag.

If the intention were to cultivate a sense of family or community, I could wear a deep brown dress in a flowing style. I would pair it with a square-face watch and neutral tones.

If the intention were to be more organized and strive for excellence, I would use designer clothing, accessories and unique artistic jewelry in round or oval shapes. I would wear deep-tone fluid fabrics and round-toed shoes.

The importance of creating and maintaining the Fashion Feng Shui® vision board

To recognize opportunities that present themselves in one's life and align with the dreams and deeper desires that can come up, the vision board is your most important tool. It is a collage of your creative self, and along with your clothing, it underpins your intention in the Fashion Feng Shui® journey.

The vision board is your best friend and, like friendship, grows and improves with time. Creation of the board is the first step. I believe a tangible board is best as opposed to a virtual one, as the process of acquiring photo images and items to include on the board takes on a greater significance if they are handled physically.

Look at the vision board on a regular basis. You may want to make changes, refine, improve and add to it. If this doesn't occur randomly, make a time (write in your diary) weekly, monthly, as a prompt to do this.

Don't worry too much about pushing your intentions to manifest themselves. Believe and leave it to a greater power to take care of the how!

Little hinges that swing big doors

Here are some motivational words from various sources that have meant a great deal to me:

Your mind is a powerful thing. When you fill it with positive thoughts, your life will start to change.

The best way to predict the future is to create it.
In order to succeed, we must first believe that we can.

Where intention goes, energy flows.

So often we do what convention dictates instead of following our hearts.

Some people don't always know what they want in life, so life leads them by the nose from day to day, month to month, year to year.

First decide what you don't want; this will free you up to think of what you do want.

Practice enthusiastic action—do it now!

Acquire knowledge and act on it to stimulate desire.

Each time we say "we can't" do something, we unconsciously block the possibility; if we change the word to "can," we reinforce a positive conscious intention.

Have an inspirational dream, have a dozen. It doesn't matter— anything is possible! It can be simple, spiritual, political, financial, travel-related—anything you like!

Look outside of the box; don't live your life on autopilot.

"What lies behind us and what lies before us are but tiny matters compared with what lies within us."

~ Ralph Waldo Emerson

Beverley Eve Cole
CIP, FFSM

Color and Image Professional,
Fashion Feng Shui® Master Facilitator
Auckland, New Zealand

A Confident and Authentic You

+64 9 8178682
bev@beverleycole.co.nz
www.beverleycole.co.nz

Beverley Cole was born in Liverpool England, lived and studied in Canada, returned to Liverpool during the Swinging Sixties and then emigrated from the UK to New Zealand. She is now based in New Zealand, where she operates her business, Beverley Cole Colour and Image.

From being a medalist in the Miss Great Britain Beauty Pageant, through modeling and direct marketing up to her work in the skincare and cosmetic industry, Beverley has had a lifelong passion for personal color and image. Her objective as an image consultant and trainer is to empower her clients to become authentic, stylish and confident.

She has been instrumental in shaping the New Zealand image industry, not only helping the industry move forward through her own work, but also encouraging and motivating colleagues. She has done this most obviously as vice president of the New Zealand Federation of Image Professionals, of which she was a founder member.

Since 1985, Beverley has trained over 500 consultants, many of whom have been inspired to pursue their own rewarding careers. Beverley's past company, Fashion Academy (NZ) Ltd., was registered and accredited by New Zealand Qualifications Authority as a private training establishment.

These days Beverley attends conferences, seminars and workshops both locally and internationally to ensure that she continues to be on the cutting edge of her profession.

Beverley's background includes fashion, hairdressing, makeup artistry, beautician, image consulting, interior decorating, Feng Shui, Fashion Feng Shui®, virtual training, nutrition, sales and marketing and accounting.

Your Personal Branding Strategy
With Fashion Feng Shui®

By Sabine Kaufmann

"You cannot not communicate."

~ *Paul Watzlawick*

People often think personal branding is a way to communicate some image of themselves to the world, an image different from who they really are. In that sense, personal branding becomes more about the role they wish to play, rather than an expression of their true authentic self.

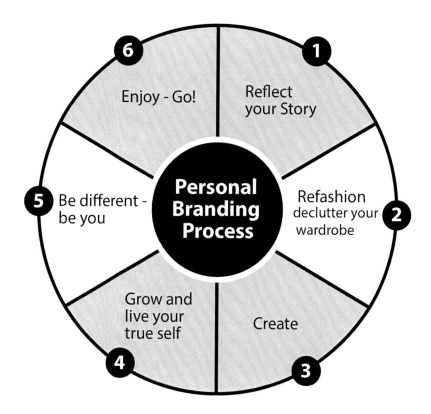

6 — Enjoy - Go!

1 — Reflect your Story

2 — Refashion declutter your wardrobe

3 — Create

4 — Grow and live your true self

5 — Be different - be you

Personal Branding Process

But in my philosophy to personal branding it follows that you cannot be successful in your business or private life until you express your true authentic self, inside and outside. Personal branding is therefore about genuine self-expression. Only then can you find your true value, and that is what brings you the happiness, success and health you have been seeking your entire life.

Step 1: Reflect
Mirror, mirror on the wall…

The first step in the personal branding process is reflection. That means taking a good look at your reflection as well as then reflecting on what you see and want you don't see—yet.

In today's world, the way others see us has a real impact on our lives. Good personal branding does not happen overnight. It is how we interact with others over time. It is how we communicate through spoken and written words, including our posts on social media platforms such as Facebook, Instagram, LinkedIn, Pinterest and Twitter. These are all forms and forums of interaction that reflect our brand.

Personal branding, moreover, is created through the combination of different elements. They include:
- Your talents: everybody is uniquely gifted. Maybe you don't recognize your own talents, but I am sure you have them.
- Your values: everybody has values that are important to them. We feel confident when we have people around us who hold the same values. Therefore, when choosing a company to work for, it is important that you can identify with their core values; otherwise, you won't feel at ease or be able to reach your goals.
- Your passions: what do you love doing? In an ideal scenario, you can combine your work and your passion.

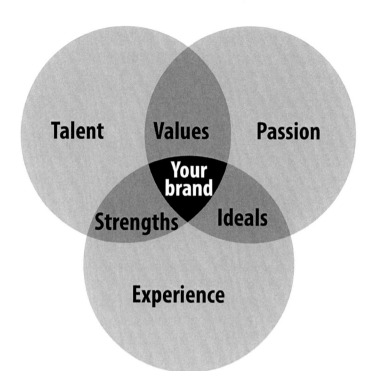

- Your strengths: everybody has strengths, even though we tend to more easily recognize our weaknesses. So what do you excel at? Ask your friends or colleagues for feedback should you find it difficult to identify this yourself. We often do certain things without hesitation or doubt, but do not perceive it as a reflection of strength. But make no mistake—it is! What for you might be easy to do would leave someone else struggling.
- Your ideals: what are your ideals in life? What is it you strive for? Along with your values, it is essential that your work reflect your ideals. This fulfills us.
- Your experiences: every day of your life is filled with new experiences that define you. Whether they are good or bad, it is the combination of these experiences that makes you unique. Only you and you alone have experienced these moments.

Building trust is the key. It doesn't matter what your profession is. We make decisions every single day that affect how we feel about ourselves. Our preferences and our choices dictate our personal tastes. We learn to trust ourselves and our choices.

So, to continue reflecting, answer the following questions about yourself:
- Who are you? (Just the hard facts, please.)
- What do you love to do?
- Do others ask for your advice? If so, when?
- How do you want to been seen by others?

"Don't dress for the job you have—dress for the job you want to have."

~ *Giorgio Armani*

Step 2: Re-fashion

So, how do others see you? Is there a gap between their perception and how you feel about yourself? At the core is your body's coloring and shape. The next stop is your closet. What choices have you made that fit you visually today and that are an expression of all the collected information of you, now?

In the second and the third phases of this process, I work with my clients to create a "capsule wardrobe." That is, a collection of clothes and accessories that reveal confidence in the client across the different environments of home, work, play.

Your talents, values, passions, strengths, ideals and experiences make you who you are. To brand yourself successfully, you need to communicate all these elements to others. This is how they will discover you and how you will discover them.

Let's go back to Watzlawick's quote: "You cannot not communicate." Have you heard about the first impression? First impressions are unavoidable. They happen unconsciously and within the first seconds of meeting someone. Likeable or not? This classification of friend or enemy goes back to the beginning of time. This skill was crucial for survival. When you spend more time with someone you just met, you might figure out why you came to this conclusion. Leaving a positive first impression of yourself with others is also a positive first impression for the company to hire you.

What we actually say when making the first impression has only a small fraction of influence.
- 40 percent is influenced by your voice and intonation.
- 50 percent is influenced by non-verbal signals, including body language and clothing.
- 10 percent is influenced by the actual message.

Voice

When you are relaxed and confident, your voice will be too. Moreover, it is important to choose your words wisely. Instead of "Nice to meet you," you can say, "It is an honor to have the opportunity to meet you, Mr. Smith." Try to be different from the norm. Say things in a way that reveals your personality and how you interact with people in general.

Body language

Your body is always speaking, even when your mouth isn't. So be careful what you think! What you think is reflected in your body language. And the opposite is of course true too. If your posture suggests insecurity or lack of confidence, you will think or feel the same. If you put your hands in your pockets or fold your arms when you talk to someone, you send a negative, closed-off message.

Facial expression

A facial expression is the result of movements made on your face, including by your eyes, mouth, forehead and eyebrows. Because many of the movements are involuntary or unconscious, it is difficult to control your facial expression. People who have undergone too many Botox sessions barely convey expression anymore—we can no longer read their faces, and the face stops reinforcing spoken statements. However, if the look created by Botox is too dramatic, it appears exaggerated and the conversation resembles a theatre-like performance. The impression that it leaves is one of dishonesty.

Hands

The hands create a never-ending waterfall of words, whether they are still or in motion. A non-moving hand may show insecurity or fear. As tension rises, the same impression of insecurity surfaces by fiddling with a pen, a ring or a necklace. Playing with jewelry or hair is often observed in women, while men might tug at their beard or rub their chin.

Posture and attitude

Your weight should be evenly distributed on both legs. Feet, hips and shoulders should vertically align. Shoulders should be straight and relaxed, arms hanging loosely to the side of the body. Look straight ahead, ready to make eye contact.

Clothing

The first impression our clothing leaves is key. People first see our clothes, not our abilities, personality or intelligence. Your outfit is therefore the statement you make even before you have said a word. Clothing always has a signaling effect. How you choose to dress not only conveys how importantly or unimportantly you take yourself, but also reveals your attitude toward others. Many people will interpret poor dress choice as disrespect for the occasion and the company. Additionally, you risk the assumption that your careless appearance implies you are careless in other areas, too. Consider all the issues where you are currently struggling. Clothes speak. And the right clothing can convey trust.

Now, let's take a trip through the closet. What do you see? A full closet but still nothing to wear? Please select the pieces that you love and those clothes that you wear every day. What do these items have in common?

Color, texture, pattern? Do you wear them in your free time, for work or both? Step 2 is all about reorganizing your wardrobe.

Step 3: Create

Feng Shui is the ancient art of placement. The Eastern principle of harmony and balance in your environment inspires a happier, healthier and more successful life to achieve your goals. Fashion Feng Shui® focuses on how you dress to live the life of your dreams. The process is a journey on which you discover the clothes that fulfill and flatter your spirit. By complimenting your body's shape and coloring, you bring it in synch with your lifestyle—so as to fortify you and help you nurture your desires.

If you compare this process to more conventional style consulting, where clothing is chosen to suit an individual's appearance and the occasion, you'll see how Fashion Feng Shui® helps tell your unique story. Bringing elemental harmony into your dressing encourages you to express who you really are within your surroundings. A collective expression of your experiences, talents, strengths, ideals, values and passions is revealed along the journey toward your authentic self. Your story, your way, your look together build your personal brand.

How do others see you? Is there a gap between how they perceive you and how you feel about yourself? At the core is your body, its shape and coloring; the next stop is your closet. So ask yourself: what choices have I made that fit me, visually speaking, today? What choices are a reflection of all the information collected about me, now?

One of the most important dress code rules is that clothing fits the person, the location and the occasion. Style emerges when an outfit flatters all three. Your choice of clothing signals what others can expect from you. Think of some famous brands—they must deliver their product just as they promise they will. That's how you have to create your own personal brand.

I recommend that your basic wardrobe, whether for business or leisure, be built to honor your essence and appearance. The big advantage to taking this approach is that you'll be self-confident in any situation. You'll look and feel fabulous without even having to look in the mirror. Note: a technique to appear trustworthy is to match your shirt or top with the color of your eyes.

A basic wardrobe includes:

- Coats
- Jackets
- Shirts
- Trousers
- Dresses
- Skirts

Colors and patterns should compliment your natural complexion, hair and of course personality. Cuts should flatter your appearance. Your body shape sometimes may get in your way, but remember that you can always alter the appearance of your body though dressing techniques. Colors, patterns, textures and fabrics help integrate your essence, your lifestyle and your intention.

Fragrances are a wonderful way to express your inner self. Maybe you already have a signature scent, one you have used for years. Have you ever smelled a fragrance and instantly remembered some person or place? You feel suddenly connected with him or her or that spot. A well-chosen scent represents you; it feels like it was created for you.

Accessories can also be used to express your intentions, highlight your look and connect you with your audience. Basic accessories include:

- Glasses
- Belts
- Hats
- Earrings

- Scarves
- Jewelry
- Watches
- Tights

The same rule applies for accessories. Use patterns that link to the Fashion Feng Shui® element you wish to add in your life. This is also a great way to express your personality. Be sure the textures and fabrics feel good because then you will feel comfortable in your movements. For jewelry, choose pieces based on the right element for you. The goal is to find a personal way to integrate all five elements in your wardrobe for a balanced life.

The element of **Water** helps cultivate creative expression, original ideas and spiritual exploration. Water accessories represent individuality, freedom and spirituality. Use black or dark tones, patterns like paisley on ties and scarfs.

Photos: Accessorize, Topman, Sunglasses Shop, Orsay, Debenhams, Amara, Topshop, Littlewoods Ireland

Use the element of **Wood** to create a professional or a personal context that promotes health and wellbeing, inspired ideas, well-motivated actions and new horizons. Wood accessories represent the wish for learning, achievement, motivation and action. Use greens and blues, floral prints or stripes, ribbed and crisp textures and fabrics such as cotton, denim and linen.

Photos: Topman, Sunglasses Shop, Accessorize, Mens at Dune, Primark UK, Jigsaw, Orsay

The element of **Fire** cultivates passion, magnetism, celebrity, illumination, enthusiasm for ideas and enjoyment. Fire accessories should be worn when you are seeking attention. You can integrate purple or red tones, as well as animal prints and fabrics such as shiny silk and fur, real or faux.

Photos: Dune, Accessorize, Sunglasses Shop, Topman, Orsay, Amara

Use the element of **Earth** when you're needing comfort, more conservative ideas, sense of responsibility, wise action and stability. Earth accessories cultivate commitment, support, harmony and diplomacy. Use yellows, browns and other earth tones, checked or plaid patterns, textures that are nappy or nubby and fabrics such as flannel, tweed and raw silk.

Photos: Sunglasses Shop, Dune, Accessorize, Debenhams, Orsay, M & Co., Topman, Barbour

The element of **Metal** promotes orderliness, lofty ideas, focused action and beauty. Metal accessories should be worn when you feel ready to achieve your goals through your own sense of organization and excellence. Integrate white, pastels or metallic colors with dotted, scrolled or parchment-like patterns and fabrics such as crêpe de chine, cashmere and sateen.

Photos: Dreyfuss & Co, Dune, River Island, Sunglasses Shop, Accessorize, Next, Jaeger

Know your clients, know the field; like attracts like.

If you work in a creative, intellectual or spiritual career with academics, musicians, writers or healers, add the element of Water to your wardrobe.

If you work with coaches, lawyers, salespeople or trainers, add the element of Wood to your wardrobe.

If you work with actors, agents, hosts or speakers, add the element of Fire to your wardrobe.

If you work with assistants, therapists, mothers or politicians, add the element of Earth to your wardrobe.

If you work with organizers, curators or editors, add the element of Metal to your wardrobe.

Why? When you add a specific element to your wardrobe aligned with a particular field, people from that category begin to see themselves in you.

They are drawn to communicate with you; they feel linked to you and trust you more because you come across as similar and display the same attracting elements.

Case study: Susanne

A few years ago, Susanne's partner called and told me that he wanted to surprise her with a gift consultation. He wanted to help his girlfriend find her own style. He decided to book my Step 1 (Closet Detox), Step 2 (Image Consulting Program) and Step 3 (Personal Shopping). I explained that I wanted to give her the opportunity to meet with me, first. Her trust in our relationship is just as important as my objective point of view.

I began by visiting their office. A very elegant lady introduced herself to me. Something felt strange about the first impression. I was curious. I was escorted to the meeting room. I asked her how she felt about her partner's gift. She said that at first she was very angry and sad; she thought that it meant that he was not satisfied with her. He had surprised her with the idea the same day that I was scheduled to show up for our appointment. Still, she recognized that her habit of changing outfits several times before she left the house for work in the morning gave her partner the idea that there was an opportunity to offer his love and support.

After our initial meeting, she enthusiastically agreed to give the process a chance. I went to her home. We started with her walk-in closet. It was overwhelming. There were so many different styles, so many different stories, so many different ways to live. I helped her realize that every outfit combination tells its own story. And these stories didn't match how she talked, moved and interacted with her environment and her story. The home interior fell into the elemental categories of Water and Fire. In this process, interior design choices also tell a lot about a client's personality. At our first meeting, Susanne wore an outfit that channeled Metal.

During our closet detox session, we created a shopping list of what we should buy to complete, update or enhance her look. By going with Susanne to shop for these key pieces, I was able to point out items that would make her feel more comfortable, colors that would enhance her personality and gently break habits in her choices that didn't enrich her life. Right after that, she started to implement the new ideas in her wardrobe.

On the first day back to work, Susanne received compliments. Colleagues noted how fabulous she looked. She began to feel more confident by expressing her own unique story through her outfits. This practice deepened her relationship with her surroundings. Her authentic self matched the principles of Wood and Fire.

Case study: Kate

When Kate, an elementary school teacher, visited me, she seemed very confused and depressed. During our Q&A, I asked her to describe herself as the teacher she currently was and the kind of teacher she wanted to be. It became obvious that she had self-doubts, both personally and about whether she could still perform well in her job. She explained that the atmosphere in the classroom was tense, and she felt that current difficulties she was experiencing with the students meant they were sensing her confusion. She hoped that coming to me would give her the opportunity to revive her passion for teaching math as well as her energy and enthusiasm, in general.

I began to probe her personal life a bit to find the cause of her low energy level. Conducting an intake involves taking a litmus test of all aspects of a client's life. Kate lived with just her two cats. Her boyfriend had left her without giving a real reason. For the past two years, she hadn't dated and rarely went out. She had a lonely existence. She felt tired all the time no matter how much she slept. Her wardrobe was drab, literally colorless; she wore black like a protective shroud.

We talked about her intentions, why she had chosen to be a teacher, in the first place. She told me how she loved kids and how she loved math. When she was still in school, she had given private lessons to children and recognized how much she loved teaching. But I had to remind her: to take care of others, you must take care of yourself, too. We had our work cut out for us.

Kate had pale skin (Metal), dyed black hair (Water), blue eyes (Wood) and a soft triangle body shape (Water). Black is a color of authority, but for work with little children, it signaled too much negative energy. It was too serious to inspire them to have fun and embrace playful learning skills. The children could not see her as a figure to attach to because she generated an invisible wall. For her work with children, green, blue, yellow and red were better colors, triggering their attention. Red was especially good for math because the color generates creativity and attention at the same time. I tried to show Kate the differences between these young people in their own colorful clothes and her black uniform.

Speaking in Feng Shui language, we talked about the relationships between colors and the elements: green/blue (Wood), yellow (Earth) red (Fire).

Kate's natural essence is Earth, so I suggested she add Wood and Fire to her wardrobe to create the atmosphere she wanted for herself and her students.

After a little makeover, a new haircut and a new wardrobe, she felt much more energized and comfortable in her surroundings. The elements helped her transform her life. She found her lost passion for teaching again.

In fact, she became the kind of teacher she was ten years earlier. Kate even found a healthy relationship in which she was able to explore her newfound confidence.

Step 4: Grow—into your true self

When you start to dress according to your personality and identity, your values, ideals, strengths, experiences and passions become one with your appearance. When you live according to who you are, your unique personal skills become visible to others as well.

Step 5: Be different—but be you

Once your capsule wardrobe has been created, you feel immediately that life changes. You feel better and look better, inside and out.

Through personal branding, you show others what they can expect from you. If you are true to yourself, you are bound to find a business partner or an ideal client who is aligned with your true nature. Family, friends and others in your immediate environment start to recognize the change. I promise you, when you keep going towards your path, life will improve.

Using the Fashion Feng Shui® technique will make you feel comfortable because the clothing is linked with your personality. When you feel comfortable, you act, sit and talk naturally. The effect is to give everybody the most authentic first impression of yourself.

Step 6: Start now!

Take your time and implement these five branding steps into your process. Reflect meaningfully on every step. By the end, you will feel confident and able to find the clients you have sought after or get the job you have always wanted. Congrats—you are fab! Now follow your dreams!

> **"**Always believe in yourself, because if you don't, then who will, sweetie?"
>
> ~ *Marilyn Monroe*

Sabine Kaufmann
FFSF, WYEF

Fashion Feng Shui® Facilitator, Work Your
Element™ Facilitator, Stylist, Coach
Liechtenstein and Austria

+423 794 44 66
+ 43 676 436 64 445
hallo@image-agentur.com
about.me/sabinekaufmann
www.image-agentur.com

Sabine Kaufmann is now based in Liechtenstein, where she heads an image consulting firm. She was born in Switzerland to parents of Liechtenstein descent. She went to school in Switzerland, got married in Austria and lived there until travels took her to Bali, Bangkok, Los Angeles, New York, Vancouver, Rome, Paris, Toronto and London. For many years, Sabine toured the world and was exposed to constant changes in environments, organizations, people and languages. These amazing experiences led her to the aesthetics of Eastern culture and the "invisible forces" at work within personal spaces.

Sabine Kaufmann has a degree in communications from Zurich University of Applied Sciences. She is a member of the AICI New York chapter and more recently, studied Fashion Feng Shui® with Sue Donnelly in London and Andrea Dupont in Boston.

Combining Fashion Feng Shui® with her experience of working for clients in the financial sector, retail sales and luxury goods and her passion for travel and faraway cultures, Sabine became an expert at dressing the personality—and this is what she does on a daily basis. She counsels both individual and corporate clients on appearance, behavior, communication skills, etiquette and international protocols.

Hair Color and Style

Your Essence and Your Intention

By Lola Intagliata Avgoustatos

As a hair colorist and an appearance coach, for many years in the business now, I regularly give my opinion about what hair and clothing would work best for my clients. My tool used to be personal color analysis. The method was simple: I would hold color swatches up to a client's face and when certain hues complimented her skin and eyes, I noted which season they were categorized under and then voilà! This would be my client's official season and she would be advised to wear clothes made of fabrics incorporating these colors. Seasons were based on color palettes and simply categorized as winter, spring, summer and autumn. For years, this served as a great way to guide women toward their best personal look.

Now as I reflect on that method of color analysis, I am aware that color has energy. As such, color should be embraced with a mindful, self-reflexive sense of who you are, what kind of energy you possess and what kind of energy you seek. When trying to bring balance to your total image using the techniques of Fashion Feng Shui®, start with your hair color. Some of you may have even used these techniques when choosing your hair color without even knowing.

In this chapter, I explore the methodology of Fashion Feng Shui® and show you how it connects to hair color choice and, in turn, how it has the power to guide the direction of your total image.

Hair-as-a-trigger journey

Long before I started my career in the beauty industry, I experienced the interplay between hair color and Fashion Feng Shui®. My example couldn't be better, or any more personal. I am the daughter of a hairdresser (as they were called way back when), so I grew up in a beauty parlor. As a kid, I remember watching my mother perform her "magic" on clients. Every Saturday morning, women came to have their hair set in rollers and then sat patiently under the hooded hairdryers. I remember their faces' red glow, warmed from the heat on their heads. It was a ritual for these women. Week after week, they would come in for "a roll and tease," as they called it in the industry. Thank goodness the blow dryer was invented!

My mother was an artist, a perfectionist and a doer, and she came to America for a better life. In her home country, she had been a hairstylist; in America, the first obstacle she faced was the language barrier. This did not stop her though. My mother set up a salon chair and portable dryer in the living room of our home and began to work. It didn't matter that she couldn't speak English; her work did all the talking for her talent. Her clientele quickly grew to such high numbers that she was able to open her own salon. My mother, a tall striking woman with black hair teased up into a French twist, began her journey.

In Fashion Feng Shui®, black reflects intuition, self-expression and independence. Was it a coincidence that her hair color was black at a time when these traits were coursing through her? After a year of her black hair period, my mother came home with brown hair. The next week it was red hair. Then the following week came yellow blonde hair (it was not very pretty, I might add). My siblings and I  didn't understand what was happening. We didn't understand that the process of extreme hair color change has to be done in phases. My mother's ultimate goal was to have platinum blonde hair.

It wasn't until I started to write this chapter that I realized that Fashion Feng Shui® was present in so many ways during her transition. I now understand why she wanted that hair color. Platinum blonde hair gives the energy of Metal and Fire, which together evoke beauty, excellence, quality and elegance. Fire's energy says: "Here I am, world. I have arrived!" My mother must have felt that she had made her mark and wanted everyone to know it. To this day, everyone remembers how dramatically she wore that hair color.

How does your hair color make you feel?

Hair color has an energy that can reflect your essence and your intention. I came to realize that my mother has a Water/Fire essence. She remained a platinum blonde for ten years. When she sold her salon, she became a redhead. Why? Because her intentions had changed, so her hair color and style did too. Looking back now, I so clearly see how her journey truly correlated with her intentions, which were reflected in her hair color changes. Red communicates an innate love of life, being adaptable and open for new and exciting possibilities—and that is exactly where my mother was when she sold her salon. To this day, she remains a redhead!

> **"** They may forget what you said—but they will never forget how you made them feel."
>
> ~ *Carl W. Buehner*

Salons are a hub for personal expression. People need to feel connected to their stylist. They share their thoughts and feelings there, and it is the place where they exchange personal stories. Each hairstylist will attract a certain type of client—it is the law of attraction: like attracts like.

Have you ever stopped to consider why you have stayed with your stylist all this time? What is it about her or him that keeps you connected? Could it be that Fashion Feng Shui® is at work? Does your stylist have a Water essence: the imaginative, intellectual self-expressive type? Or Wood: the action-oriented, assertive, health-focused initiator? Maybe Fire: a captivating, passionate, entertaining and uplifting person? Or possibly Earth: a grounded, nurturing, traditional, committed and reliable person. Or Metal: a natural leader who is organized, has a keen eye for detail and is always appropriate and reserved? Which of these energies resembles your own?

A major hair color company recently ran a campaign that challenged salon owners to rethink how to address their clients' needs. The campaign involved a questionnaire asking stylists to mark down some notable characteristics of their clients: namely, face shape, current hair color, personality type the client would be categorized as based on selective criteria, including clothing personality. Never before had a hairstylist been asked to take all of those things into consideration when changing a client's hair color. Immediately, I recognized the Fashion Feng Shui® approach in this exercise.

Let me explain. Fashion Feng Shui® helps you discover your essence— that is, who you are at your core—and helps you learn how to express your intention through color, style and texture. Intention is what is easily recognized by people you encounter. Remember: you only get 30 seconds to make a first impression, so what we show the world we are, at any given time, is in fact our intention.

For example, a female corporate executive goes through a life change and is now a fulltime stay-at-home mom. As an executive, her intention was expressed as Metal. Her hairstyle was a very elegant, sleek, short bob. But her new position, as a stay-at-home mom, has changed her intention. Now her hairstyle has gotten longer, and she has added layers to her hair. This gives her hairstyle a more relaxed, traditional feel that expresses as Earth.

Does one's hair color and style reflect their changing intention? Many times it does, but the person does not understand that a deeper change—one of intention—also has taken place, and it is more than just a new hair color or style that reflects that change.

In Fashion Feng Shui®, we see Water as the Philosopher, Wood as the Pioneer, Fire as the Pleasure Seeker, Earth as the Peacemaker and Metal as the Perfectionist.

If you came into my salon, you would be welcomed with a robe and a cup of coffee or tea. I would then ask you these 10 questions (for which there is no right or wrong answer):

1. What was your hair color when you were a teenager?
2. What hair colors have you had in your life?
3. Did you like any of those hair colors and, if so, why?
4. What do you love most about your current hair color?
5. If you could have any hair color, what would it be?
6. What is it about that hair color that makes you want to have it?
7. Whose hairstyle do you admire, and why?
8. How much time do you want to spend styling your hair?
9. What would you like your hairstyle and color to say about you?
10. Do you think your current style and color represent your intention?

I took two of my clients through this process and would like to share their hair-as-a-trigger journeys with you.

Case study: Julia

Julia is a professional woman working in the financial industry. She is highly organized and very effective at her job. Her hair is fine in texture,

and she prefers to keep it short. We had been coloring and highlighting her hair a neutral dark blonde and adding soft gold highlights.

One day, Julia came in and said: "I want a change." These are the words every hair stylist loves to hear; it gives us the power of carte blanche. So the old me would have said: "Oh, let's put some dark lowlights for contrast. It's fall, you know, and I think that would bring out your blue eyes." But the new me felt the need to intervene with Fashion Feng Shui®. Binging it into the decision-making process, I needed to understand why she wanted change. So I asked: "Julia, why the change? Is there something you want to attract in your life now?" She said: "Yes, I want to have more fun!" To that I replied: "Well, what does fun mean to you?" Her response was: "I want to be noticed more, I want excitement!"

I immediately began considering her perfect color using Fashion Feng Shui® principles. Julia was describing her intention to me. But in Fashion Feng Shui® we explore our essence and through that find our intention.

I therefore explained to Julia that we were going to evoke her intention through her hair's style, color and texture.

Fire is the element we draw from when we want to attract fun and excitement. Hair colors that reflect Fire range from shades of standard red to copper-red, and Julia went "red!" I know sometimes women don't like hearing the words "red" and "hair" in the same sentence (perhaps for fear of looking too *I Love Lucy*), but as the saying goes: "blondes may have more fun, but redheads get it done!" As you can see Julia was so delighted with her new look and even more ecstatic about the journey it was going to take her on.

I like to call our hair-as-a-trigger moments a journey because if we ever stop to look at the photos from our life, wow, what a story all of those moments tell!

Case study: Kathy

Kathy is also a professional. She holds a high management position in the medical industry. Her natural hair color is dark brown. Over the years, she has played with different dark shades, dabbling with black hair at one time and more recently maintaining a dark brown color with lighter highlights; she was attracted to the dramatic contrast between the light highlight and her dark base color.

For some time, Kathy's stylist at my salon maintained a similar look of a dark base color with light highlights. The stylist decided to change her own hair color to a light ash blonde. Witnessing her stylist's change triggered Kathy to also make a transition from dark hair with light highlights, to a bright light blonde. After three months, I decided to sit down with Kathy and explore how she really felt about her new blonde hair color. I believed that at its core, the decision to change her hair color correlated with a change in her intention.

My exploration of Kathy's hair-as-a-trigger journey began with a discussion of her dark hair color period. When asked about that time, Kathy said: "I loved a dramatic look, but never wanted red hair. Lola, I didn't want to look natural and anyway, who wants natural hair color! I loved the dark for the drama it gave me!"

What Kathy did not realize was that she was actually describing to me the elemental archetype of Water/Fire. Water hair color is black to dark brown, and when someone puts contrasting highlights in it, they do so for its dramatic effect, which equates to Fire. I then asked her why she made the sudden decision to change from her dark color to such a light blonde. Kathy explained: "The older you get, I feel the braver you become. I don't care what people think. I like to say, 'don't like, don't look.' Last year was a very challenging year for me. There were medical issues, sad family events and the fact that I was getting older. I felt like I just crashed and I wanted to move on from the past. I felt I needed a new start. When I saw that my stylist had changed her color from dark to light, I knew that was the hair color I wanted. I needed that extreme change! My stylist was shocked, but never asked why (which was OK), and did exactly what I asked."

The process of changing hair color was long for Kathy, and it took two visits to achieve her ultimate color. In the end, she was delighted. There was a sparkle to her that was missing before. When asked how her new hair color made her feel, Kathy simply beamed. She said: "This color makes me feel like I have a new platform to start from. A renewed energy I got out of feeling stuck. I no longer feel old; I look forward to the new. I felt the dark hair was holding me back; changing my outward appearance made me able to start over. This different appearance has given me a renewed sense of self."

I then went on to ask Kathy which of the statements below resonated with her the most in the past. This was a method to establish her past intention.

- I express myself freely.
- I initiate change.
- I live, I laugh, I love.
- I am grounded and centered.
- I am organized and meticulous.

She was stuck between two, Water and Fire, and after thinking for a minute, chose "I express myself freely." The hair-as-a-trigger color for "I express myself freely" is Water, which equates to dark hair. Kathy maintained her natural dark color for years though added high-contrast highlights, reflecting her intentional flairs of Fire. Kathy was delighted to finally understand that she was actually just being her authentic self!

Next, I asked her to look at the same questions but with a focus on her present intention. She chose "I initiate change." She said: "It is very rewarding for me when I get to experience that 'AHA' moment with people." She immediately felt that she understood what her actions were doing for her and why she started to feel renewed. Kathy then went on to say that after her hair color changed to blonde: "People ask[ed], did you always want to be a blonde. I said: 'No, I never wanted to be a blonde. I knew I wanted a change, an extreme change, and

I want to start something new." I explained to her how her choice of blonde hair color reflects the intention of Wood, resembling the change she initiated in her life and the vitality it gave her. Kathy did choose wisely!

Gray hair—to be or not to be!

Women sometimes like the romantic idea of letting their hair go gray. Is there an age when one should? Well, ask yourself these questions: Do I want to go gray as a trend, or do I just want to be unique or free? Your answer will lead you down the path of discovering whether this choice is about your intention or your essence. There are many shades of gray hair, and we all don't inherit the same shade of gray color.

Many of us have asked that question of ourselves over and over again, especially when we just colored our hair and two weeks later we can see the whites growing in again. Gray hair can be a fashion trend or a way of life.

When Essential Color™ expert Donna Cognac went through this trans-formation, I asked her the following questions:

- How often did you change your hair color in the past? ("Never. I only started coloring to cover gray and never changed the color.")
- Do you feel it correlated to your intention at the time? ("Yes. I never lusted after red or blonde hair, or even streaks. I guess my intention was to look and be natural. I also enjoyed the fact that the darker color made my light skin look lighter. The contrast suited that little bit of drama in me.")
- How has going gray made you feel? ("Brave. Mature. Secure. Elegant.")
- Does it express your intention or essence? ("It does express my intention. It's being a maverick when everyone else is coloring their hair (Water—Uniqueness). Another key factor

that I think of is Earth (big part of my essence), as being very pragmatic and natural, so this fits my essence nicely.")

I posed the question to hairstylist Deborah DiMeglio: As a hair stylist, what are your thoughts about women letting their hair go gray? She replied: "If you're going to go gray, you must have a fabulous hairstyle!"

Gray hair is a universal essence. It can be introspective, an achievement, pragmatic, captivating and elegant. Will it be your intention someday?

You have now read about the lives of three women, and how hair has played a role in their journeys. It is time for you to take a similar journey. Go back and look at pictures of yourself through the years. Lay them side-by-side, reflecting on the times those pictures represent from your life.

Can you see what your intention was during that time, or has your look in the pictures not changed at all? Remember the archetypes and what they represent. Was your hairstyle like...

- Water: asymmetrical, wavy or avant-garde?
- Wood: layered or shaggy and able to move freely?
- Fire: short, pixy, punk or angular?
- Earth: consistent, a layered bob or square in shape?
- Metal: sleek, elegant, geometric or a blunt bob?

See how Fashion Feng Shui® was present in your life. Also, think of what your intention is now. Here is a chart I have created to help guide you on your own hair-as-a-trigger journey. Let it help you reflect your authentic self through your hair color and total image.

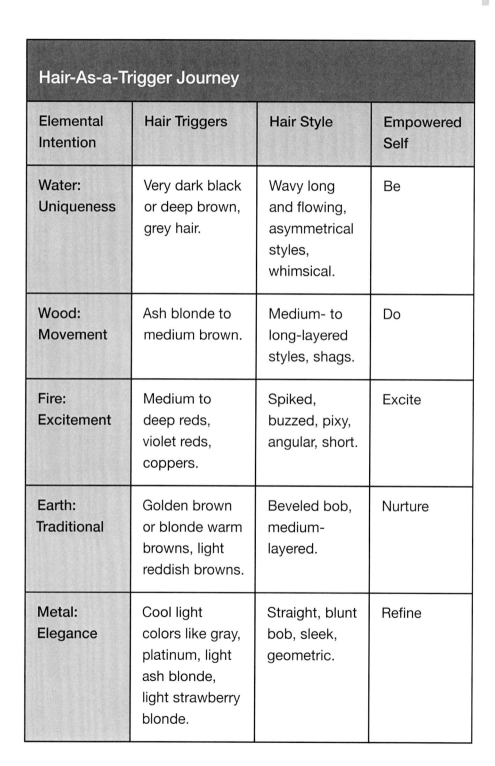

Hair-As-a-Trigger Journey

Elemental Intention	Hair Triggers	Hair Style	Empowered Self
Water: Uniqueness	Very dark black or deep brown, grey hair.	Wavy long and flowing, asymmetrical styles, whimsical.	Be
Wood: Movement	Ash blonde to medium brown.	Medium- to long-layered styles, shags.	Do
Fire: Excitement	Medium to deep reds, violet reds, coppers.	Spiked, buzzed, pixy, angular, short.	Excite
Earth: Traditional	Golden brown or blonde warm browns, light reddish browns.	Beveled bob, medium-layered.	Nurture
Metal: Elegance	Cool light colors like gray, platinum, light ash blonde, light strawberry blonde.	Straight, blunt bob, sleek, geometric.	Refine

Lola Intagliata Avgoustatos
AICI CEC, FFSF, WYEF

AICI Certified Image Consultant,
Executive Image Consultant, Manfredo
Curtis Associates, LLC, Fashion Feng
Shui® Facilitator, Work Your Element™
Facilitator, Essential Color™ Professional,
Salon Founder/Owner
West Hempstead, New York,
United States

Clear Skin, Inc.
lola@appearance-coaching.com
appearance-coaching.com

Lola Intagliata was born in Athens, Greece, and immigrated as a child to the United States with her family. She has been involved in the beauty industry her whole life. Her mother owned a hair salon, where Lola had her first experiences as a hair colorist and esthetician. She later went on to further her education at Christine Valmy and opened her own salon at the age of 21.

Since then, Lola has worked as a hairstylist, a colorist, a makeup artist, an esthetician, a Color Me Beautiful consultant, an Essential Color™ professional consultant and a Fashion Feng Shui® Facilitator. Intrinsically, she understands the science behind hair color and hair. Her remarkable skillset has attracted clients from a broad range of careers and backgrounds, relying on Lola to recreate their image from head to toe. Lola's clients range from top executives of Fortune 500 companies across the US to everyday women who want to revamp or recreate their style.

Lola, at her core, is a coach in many forms. She leads her life team by example, running a business, raising three amazing children and coaching varsity girls' soccer. A team always has a great co-captain, and her husband has been her biggest supporter and is a cornerstone of her success. Her passion for coaching combined with her expertise as a colorist, esthetician and image consultant is what led her to become a Fashion Feng Shui® Facilitator and an appearance coach. The transformative experience of looking your best drives Lola's evolving passion for image consulting and education.

As Lola has been known to say: "Color can be a catalyst for success." And: "'Team' is the foundation of my life's philosophy."

Accessorizing with Fashion Feng Shui®

By Cindy Nytko

According to Merriam-Webster, an accessory is "an object or device not essential in itself but adding to the beauty, convenience, or effectiveness of something else." Clothing and accessories tell people a lot about us. They give direction to an overall look, enhance our presentation, convey an image and add visual conversation for how we want to be seen by the world.

Accessories can take on a variety of shapes, colors and designs, and selection is a key process for men and women alike. Many of us choose accessories on a whim, because they are fashionable or perhaps because we have received them as a gift. There are a variety of reasons why we own accessories, but not all accessories get worn. Just like our clothing, we may love some more than others. We might not even like some, but feel that we have to wear them for various, often emotional, reasons.

Let me introduce the five elements into your accessory closet: Water, Wood, Fire, Earth and Metal. Each of these elements is endowed with color, shape, pattern and texture. When you become aware of their qualities and characteristics, you are able to make more mindful accessory choices. This may be to further enhance your physical appearance, to tell your essential story or to attract something new into your life. It might even be a combination of all three!

As an inspired Feng Shui practitioner, I believe in the importance of balance, flow and harmony. The interplay between Yin and Yang continues to create variations: soft and hard, warm and cold. This produces tonal changes resulting in varying degrees of color.

When you identify with your elemental archetype, whether it's Water—The Philosopher, Wood—The Pioneer, Fire—The Pleasure Seeker, Earth—The Peacemaker or Metal—The Perfectionist, you establish a point of reference. Your essence is the energy of your spirit. It's what fulfills you—it's your personal story. By combining essence, intention and appearance, you unlock your personal style.

Adding accessories allows you to update your look, rethink your style and create flair with winning combinations. Once you are ready to formulate a plan of action, I hope some of my tips will help you to:
- Create the authentic you.
- Express yourself visually and dynamically.
- Translate an image of who you are and what you stand for.
- Have fun, and not take yourself too seriously—tomorrow's another day!

Eyeglass frames

What frames you? How do you want the world to see you, and first and foremost, how do you see yourself? Having been in the optical business for over 15 years, I guess you could say I have seen millions of frames and designed numerous frame displays. As an optician and a Fashion Feng Shui® Facilitator, my intention is to help guide you in your next selection, keeping both functionality and aesthetics in mind.

How to select glasses
Fit
- The fit is it! You instantly know what feels good. Still, have someone accompany you, especially if you can't see yourself clearly when you take your glasses off and look in a mirror. If possible, wear contact lenses that day. Glasses are an investment, so take the time to make the right decision.
- Bridge fit—which is crucial—stabilizes the frame's position on the nose. A properly sized frame and correct temple lengths (that is, the arms of the glasses) establish balance.

Bridge types
- Saddle: fits along the top and sides of the nose.
- Keyhole: vaults the top of the nose and just touches the sides.
- With or without nose pads.

Frame materials
- Plastic (also known as zyl or acetate)
- Metal
- A combination
- Rimless

Temple types
- Skull—bends at the top behind the ear, fits close to the back of the head.
- Spring Load Flex—these flex hinges are equipped with a small spring that affords the temples a greater range of motion.
- Library—similar to the skull, wider narrowing at the end to allow for a slight bend.
- Paddle—straight flat wide temples that do not bend behind the ear.
- Riding Bow—curved around the ear and extended down to the level of the ear lobe.
- Comfort Cable—similar to the riding bow, wraps around the ear but is constructed by coiled, metal or flexible cable.
- Lengths—135mm, 140mm, 145mm.
- Ornate details: check the front and side view when selecting.

Now that we have the basics down, let's take this to the next level by looking at face shapes.

Face shapes

- Round—circular shape, similar width in cheekbones and jaw.
- Heart-shaped—widest at the forehead and narrow at the chin.
- Rectangular—oblong.
- Square—four equal sides.

Now let's look at some frames to complement your face shape.

What frames best suit your face shape?

- Round face: Stick to angles. Square and rectangular frames are good choices. Temples that connect at the top of the frame front are great. Decorative temples are a plus, pulling and lifting the visual line up toward the eyes. Avoid round shapes.
- Heart-shaped face: Select frames that are stronger on the bottom. By pulling the attention down on the frame front, you're adding width to the jawline. Remember balance. You can also try oval shapes. Avoid frames that are heavy on the top that will unbalance your proportions.
- Rectangular face: Look for temples that are connected midway on the frame front or at the bottom. This positioning shortens the profile of the extended jawline. Rounded frames will also soften the angularity of the face. Avoid temples attached at the top, as they will make your jaw look longer.
- Square face: Select frames that appear more rounded. They have a softening effect on a sharply angular face. Check out lighter-weight frames. Avoid heavy frames, boxy or square.

Tip: When making selections for your eyewear, consider frames that have a slight angle next to the cheekbone area. This pulls your face up, making it appear as though you are smiling, which is of course best for a first impression. If this area drags downward next to the cheekbone, please reselect. Giving the appearance of a frown really doesn't do much for anyone!

Men's frames

"You've come a long way, baby" is an understatement when looking at the vast selection of frames now available for men. Eyewear in various designs, colors and materials is everywhere. Gone are the days when guys had such few options—along with clothes, frames are also spotlighted on the red carpet. It's just delightful to see this interplay of expression being exhibited by men and women both. "Easy on the eyes" might be an old expression, but it still holds true. Who doesn't like to look at another person who is well put-together?

Water—Artistic—Creative
The Philosopher is well matched with frames in dark tones, made of reflective materials in very imaginative and unusual styles.

Wood—Active—Energized
The Pioneer is well matched with frames in medium-to-light blues and greens, in a style that accommodates the tendency to move quickly and enjoy an active or sporty lifestyle and image.

Fire—Vibrant—Charismatic
The Pleasure Seeker is well matched with frames in red, reddish-brown, violet and purple, since high-contrasting colors are ones that get people noticed.

Earth—Nurturing—Balanced

The Peacemaker is well matched with frames in golden brown, beige, yellow and earth tones, in a style that accommodates the love of comfort and a relaxed quality.

Metal—Meticulous—Qualitative

The Perfectionist is well matched with frames that are monochromatic, in a style that shows off refined details and meticulous craftsmanship.

Now that we've looked at some frames for the guys, let's see what we have for the ladies!

Women's sunglasses

What's the fastest way to create drama? Sunglasses! This is why you see them on the runways and the red carpet. They exude a sense of mystery and intrigue, giving the beholder subtle messages.

From Lady Gaga's most outlandish costumes to the functionality and practicality of Bobbi Brown's cosmetics, the market is inundated with colors and styles.

Here are some tips that may help you in your selection of lenses:
- Lenses come in three categories: single vision, bifocal and progressives.
- Lens colors range from light brown to dark gray.
- High-fashion lenses vary from light to dark, covering a full spectrum of color.
- Full tints are solid color on the lens. Gradient tints have color at the top and fade out at the bottom.

- Polarized lenses give you the greatest protection from the sun.
- Ultraviolet protection is an absolute must. This protects the retina from harmful sunrays.

Water—Artistic—Creative
The Philosopher
Plastic—black—dark and mysterious

Wood—Active—Energized
The Pioneer
Acetate—blue—casual, sporty looks

Fire—Vibrant—Charismatic
The Pleasure Seeker
Zyl—red—wants to be noticed

Earth—Nurturing—Balanced
The Peace Maker
Plastic—beige-brown to variations of earth tones—stable and balanced

Metal—Meticulous—Qualitative
The Perfectionist
Metal or frame front with acetate— pale colors—detailed, refined

Women's frames
Water—Artistic—Creative
The Philosopher in dark tones encrusted with black crystals along the top of the frame. Swarovski crystals are included on the temples. Stunning!

Wood—Active—Energized

The Pioneer loves freedom of move-ment in blue tones. The Swarovski crystals on the side of the temples add the slightest touch of bling. Invigorating!

Fire—Vibrant—Charismatic

The Pleasure Seeker is immediately gratified wearing these red Cazel titanium frames. Dynamic!

Earth—Nurturing—Balanced

The Peacemaker feels warm and cozy in these subtle variations of warm browns, reds and yellows. Very comforting!

Metal—Meticulous—Qualitative

Pure perfection can be found in the metal, high-end stylization of this Tura frame. Refined orchestration in the temples. Exquisite!

Belts

Belts are the perfect add-on for your wardrobe. Besides offering func-tionality, they emphasize your waist and can create different interesting effects. Layering multiple skinny belts, positioned to slant off to the side, is just one way to add a little pizzazz to an outfit. The prints and textures are in themselves little works of art. And so are the buckles—take a minute to really look at them.

From metallic-sheen leathers to zebra-print fabrics, the array of belts is as wide as your imagination. So, let's examine them, shall we?

Water — Artistic — Creative

The Philosopher is well matched with belts in dark colors, brown and black, appreciating sculpted details on a belt buckle.

Wood — Active — Energized

The Pioneer is well matched with belts in blue and green, among other shades found in nature, appreciating designs that suggest action and motion.

Fire — Vibrant — Charismatic

The Pleasure Seeker is well matched with belts in animal prints and shades of red or high contrasting colors, focusing on accents that draw attention.

Earth — Nurturing — Balanced

The Peacemaker is well matched with sturdy, practical belts in hues of brown and other earth tones. They may be handmade, such as woven goods.

Metal — Meticulous — Qualitative

The Perfectionist is well matched with luxurious, high-end belts in metallic colors or monochromatic finishes, appreciating fine details, such as buckles made from the same material as the rest of the belt.

Tip: If you do not have a tiny waist but want to wear a belt, try getting a wide, oversized one that can go on the hips. It can be worn conventionally, with the buckle in the center, or off to the side.

By positioning a belt like this, you draw focus from the waist and to the angularity of the belt. Give it a try—you just might like it, especially if you are Water!

Purses

Purses are no longer just a place to stash your wallet, makeup bag, tissues, keys, cell phone and pens. They are key design pieces to any wardrobe, and they often cost accordingly. Pick up any fashion magazine and they will readily list bags retailing for thousands and thousands of dollars. If that's in your budget, fine. If not, look around at some other discount retailers that might have something closer to what you can afford.

Here are some styles to consider:
- Clutch
- Wristlet
- Shoulder bag
- Cross body bag
- Single- or double-handed tote
- Evening bag

Here are two identical leather handbags in different colors, which correspond to two of the elements. The darker tan is Earth, and the lighter beige is Metal. It can be carried by the handles or over the shoulder. One reason I've highlighted this option is because I like how it is compart-

mentalized, with various sections, plus a watch and a small flashlight. Remember that if your goal is Metal (you want to be more efficient and organized), you need tools to help you stay that way.

Identifying elemental accessories

Water—Artistic—Creative: black floppy hat, flowing gauze scarf, paisley ties, chandelier earrings, beaded drawstring pouch bag.

Wood—Active—Energized: multi-functional watch (tells time, provides location and counts steps), baseball cap, cotton tee shirt, linear stripes, denim jeans, straw tote and sneakers.

Fire—Vibrant—Charismatic: red beret, diamond-printed scarf, leather ties, animal printed clutch, zebra belt, furs, eye-catching stiletto heels and pointed toes.

Earth—Nurturing—Balanced: fedora straw hat, gingham plaid scarf, tweed vest, square-faced watch, flannel pajamas, khaki chinos, madras tie, chunky heeled or flat shoes.

Metal—Qualitative—Meticulous: metallic leather heels, designer 14 carat gold watch, silk shantung suit, gold lamé pleated skirt, silver tie, cashmere sweaters and white tuxedo shirt.

Scarves and ties

What can one say about a little piece of cloth? A lot! It can give you a pop of color, a sense of direction and a little attitude. Choose a color or fabric that represents an element you need more of, or combine two elements in a fusion to redirect your visual communication. For a boost, add some of your own elemental essence and away you go with a winning ensemble.

For the sake of illustration, I have selected a 20 x 20 scarf to demonstrate colors and patterns. Various sizes in scarves can be incorporated to achieve different looks. Patterns and colors on the scarfs can also be achieved on men's neckwear. Be creative, have fun with it and play!

Black with multicolor prints:
Water and Fire fusion

Green: Wood

Red, black-and-white: Fire

Black-and-white: Metal

The substance of this scarf is silk on silk, which displays the Metal and Fire element. When two or more elements are combined, we refer to them as a fusion. The modulation of color produces a visual landscape. It is designed to express the essence and attract the attention of the Perfectionist and the Pleasure Seeker. Upscale and Vibrant!

The Philosopher engulfs herself with dark mystery and intrigue with this black, fringed shawl. Add a little Fire with a splash of red hand-embroidered flowers to intensify the drama! Creatively dramatic— Stunning!

Jewelry

No gal or guy should ever go out without a little bit of jewelry—even if it's a beautiful watch that offers functionality and a touch of class.

Categories

- Fine jewelry consists of precious metals combined with precious gemstones. These are usually high-end pieces, passed down from one family member to another.
- Costume jewelry consists of non-precious metals combined with wood, plastic or other inexpensive materials.
- High-fashion jewelry consists of a non-precious metal electroplated with karat gold or silver. It has the look of fine jewelry without the cost.

Jewelry is a great accessory and a top seller as a gift. Jewelry defines you and what you stand for. The use of the elements Water, Wood, Fire, Earth and Metal communicate a visual message. Selecting various combinations not only alter your look, but also change your image presentation. Studies show that 55% of the messages we receive are through body language! We now know your clothing is your body's most intimate environment, and using accessories and jewelry only enhance that image. I love jewelry because of its versatility—it can change your look within seconds.

Want some pep in your step? Try a little Fire from the Pleasure Seeker. Exciting, big, bold, and dramatic, displaying a kaleidoscope of color. The gal who wears this combination wants to attract and be seen. There is only one thing left—just kick up your heels and dance!

What you see here is an enhancer. This can be worn as a necklace, pendant or as a stand-alone pin. Enhancers come in an assortment of colors and styles, which can be worn on a

string of pearls, a ribbon or another type of chain. Oh, and don't forget: they can be a nice addition to a hat or an evening bag.

Metal, Metal, Metal—The Perfectionist! White clean stones nestled in between polished metal. Monochromatic and refined, with exquisite and meticulous detail. Cultivated and exciting!

Did you notice something special about this necklace? If so, I applaud you! The design element is in the shape of the Bagua, the basis of Feng Shui.

By definition, the Bagua has nine components, which correspond to the following realms:

- Career
- Skills and knowledge
- Family
- Prosperity
- Fame and fortune
- Relationship and love
- Creativity and children
- Helpful people and travel
- Health

These areas correspond to the elements, each with their own corresponding colors and shapes. Fashion Feng Shui® provides formulas to help guide your energy, especially as it pertains to your personal presentation.

As I meet new people and explore this process again and again, it never ceases to amaze me how incredibly talented you all are. Each of you has a gift that was given to you. It's time to lift the veil and walk in your own light!

Many blessings to all. Namaste!

Cindy Nytko
FFSF, WYEF

Fashion Feng Shui® Facilitator, Work Your Element™ Facilitator, Inspired Feng Shui Practitioner, International Feng Shui Guild member, artist, interior decorator, jeweler and cosmetologist.
Chicago, Illinois, United States

+1 847-849-7340
cindynytko777@gmail.com
cindyfsj.mypremierdesigns.com

Cindy Nytko was born and raised in Chicago, Illinois. Both her parents are first-generation U.S. citizens of Polish heritage. Creativity has always been a central theme for Cindy. As a child, she participated in numerous activities including ballet, volleyball, art and music. She sang with the Chicago High School Chorus accompanied by the Chicago Symphony Orchestra.

Visual composition, color and design were what Cindy craved most, no matter what form she found them in. This is why her first choice in life was to become a cosmetologist. After successfully completing that mission, she found another calling. She was awarded a scholarship to study music at Roosevelt University and another to study art at Columbus College of Art & Design. Pursuing art was a pivotal juncture in her life. Exposure to numerous artistic modalities gave her a wider platform, and she presented in exhibitions in Columbus, Chicago and New York, eventually pursuing a Bachelor of Arts at Lake Erie College.

Experience in various positions—including that of activity director, interior and showroom designer and general manager in optics—gave Cindy a wider perspective with which to view the world, in terms of physical surroundings and personal observations. This led her to study Kundalini yoga, astrology, reflexology, Chinese meridians, numerology, intuitive readings and shamanism.

Her interest in Feng Shui was piqued by a short magazine article about the ancient art. Soon she was hooked. In 2012, her Feng Shui studies began under the tutelage of Karen Rauch Carter, who studied with Nate Batoon; Cindy remains especially grateful to Professor Lin Yun for all his wisdom. One year later, she could proudly call herself an Inspired Feng Shui Practitioner. Two years later, she became a Fashion Feng Shui® Facilitator and completed the Work your Element™ business seminar as well. This, along with being accepted to the International Feng Shui Guild, has broadened her scope globally.

Cindy has always envisioned helping individuals become all they can be—inside and outside. Just think about her toolbox and what it can do for you!

The Heart of Service
Applying Fashion Feng Shui® to the Service Industry

By Cinzia Fassetta

If you are already familiar with Fashion Feng Shui®, you know that the technique is not only about North, South, East and West, or furniture placement or clearing your environment. Fashion Feng Shui® speaks of energy—and energies—and that, in turn, speaks of the very nature of humans. Energy makes up everything and everyone on Earth. Infinitely small particles are constantly rotating at an incredibly high speed to create matter. Energy pervades everything: the air we breathe, the soil we walk on, the sun warming every living being and inanimate object on this planet.

So, what does Fashion Feng Shui® have to do with that? Fashion Feng Shui® is a contemporary interpretation of the ancient art of placement as we know, understand and value it in the Western world. Fashion Feng Shui® embraces the five elements, correlating Feng Shui's focus on our surroundings with what is our most intimate environment. It is not our home, a favorite room, nor the office in which we spend most of our day… It is our clothes.

Evana Maggiore, our beloved mentor, is the source of this interpretation.

For Westerners, like me, it is a more simplified and modernized vision than the Feng Shui tradition of the Far East, and specifically of China, where it has been practiced for over 3,000 years. But still, there is plenty to what Evana did when creating this fabulous system that intertwines ancient Chinese wisdom and our very modern need to look and feel good. Through analyzing the energies of Feng Shui's five elements and pairing them with the energies of the colors, fabric and patterns we wear, she created archetypes corresponding to each element, thus also making identification easier for every one of us. And you know what?

Through the individualization of these elemental archetypes, we can easily see how Fashion Feng Shui® can be used as a way to understand people's personalities.

As I have always said and noted on styleforyoursoul.com: "It's never just about the clothes." Fashion Feng Shui® can be an excellent way to better know yourself, identifying what styles, colors, shapes and patterns suit you best on the outside. Yet, the real gift you give is getting to know yourself better on the inside. And better still, along the way you get to know others better on the inside, too.

In a world where competitiveness and globalization have made us want to be "just like everybody else, only better," Fashion Feng Shui® shows us that being yourself—who you really are at your core—is what will give you the real advantage in life. That includes in business.

An authentic you will always be a winning you.

And what is being you, yourself, the authentic you if not behaving and acting from the very deepest and wisest knowledge source you can have: your heart? Your heart is the essence of your whole being: it's where you feel, the place from which you take the wisest action, where all your sincerest and most honest words originate. It's where your broadest smiles come from and where the purest form of love can be found.

In everyday language, we often refer to "the heart of the matter," "the heart of the issue" or "the heart of the problem" to indicate the crux of something. We can also be heard saying "with my hand on my heart" or "I wear my heart on my sleeve" when there is no mask, there is nothing to hide and we speak our truth with no embellishment or excuses. "Service from the heart" is something we might hear or say when what we do in our business affects people at a deep level and personally. This may often be said or heard about work in a service-based industry, such as health care, personal and home services or hospitality and travel.

As for my own working life, I have been a travel agent, hotel staff, restaurant staff, an airline agent, a shipping agent, a personal shopper and a wardrobe consultant. In the last two positions, my job was explicitly to help clients look and feel better by staying authentic and true to themselves. Using Fashion Feng Shui® gave me the chance to dive deep into their essence, intention and appearance and honor each aspect of their being by connecting to the energies of the five elements. In doing so, I could help my clients create their own very true style that felt right for their soul.

This is all part of what I call "the heart of service." It is what motivates me to spread a message of love and care in connecting with the world, in my personal and professional lives. Fashion Feng Shui® for the heart of service is a way to tap into ourselves and the powerful energies we are made of. We learn how to connect and communicate as our most authentic and true selves with the world around us.

Actually, you are always in the service industry whenever and wherever you "serve" a guest or a client, making them feel good, cared for or better. And, though you are not be paid for it, you serve loved ones every day. So what benefits are there for your heart of service in Fashion Feng Shui®? The five elemental archetypes—and consequently every human being who identifies with any of them—each have a unique heart of service. It is expressed through the energy pertaining to the essence of their main element. Let me explain.

If you are a **Philosopher**, your elemental energy is **Water**. It will make you very deep, always sensitive to the meaning and symbolism of words, situations and objects. Philosophers can meaningfully reflect on what surrounds them and how they can be of service in unusual and unique ways to others. They always will be found marching to the sound of their own drum.

As a Philosopher, your heart of service will not manifest in the usual client-service provider relationship. Rather, it will lie in the deep understanding of what your skills are and in your calm, patient attitude. You will take your time, never hurrying anyone to discuss an issue or situation, instead letting things flow. Still, you will dig deep to get to the heart of a matter, without leaving anything unexplored. You find your bliss when discussing great ideas with clients, coworkers and associates. You inspire them to strive for the best. If you are in the service industry, you are for sure the creative working on a new, original brand and assessing the company values behind it.

If you are a **Pioneer**, with the elemental energy of **Wood**, you are very proactive and quick in responding to any inquiry or request for help.

Your heart of service lies in finding new and innovative ways to be of service or how to serve your clients, guests and loved ones. At the same time, you make sure things evolve and do not stagnate, promoting tangible improvements, growth and evolution in everything you do.

As a Pioneer, you are particularly sensitive to challenges surrounding new things and new issues. The presence of Wood makes you want to focus on expanding as part of the solution; for you, expansion is a solution that always brings growth, a breath of fresh air and innovation. Respect for nature and its rhythms and new beginnings inform the way you use and wear your heart of service. If you are in the service industry, such as in hospitality, your delight and brilliance will be in finding new and innovative ways to pamper your guests and communicate with them. You will be inclined to use environmentally friendly channels, techniques and products.

If you are a **Pleasure Seeker**, your heart of service is all about relation-ships that make you feel good and help others feel good too. **Fire** is your elemental energy, compelling you to always look for the happy, fun side of the issue. If you have an Essence of Fire, being in an industry such as travel and hospitality or retail, where you must relate to people at some of their happiest moments, is just the fuel to keep you running.

A Pleasure Seeker will be in his or her element when dealing with the public. This entails interacting, listening, receiving and in any way open-ing his or her heart to make someone happy or have them join in on a circle of joyful people. You might be an effective guest relations manager who ensures clients are always satisfied with the products and services you provide and that your company (be it a hotel, a travel agency or an airline) has not only satisfied customers, but raving fans as well!

A **Peacemaker** has a heart of service that focuses on being nurturing and taking care of everyone who needs it. **Earth** is your elemental energy, meaning work in education, healthcare and counseling can take you to the height of happiness, motivation and success. The nurturing nature of the Earth element is what makes excellent and satisfied therapists, educators, teachers, nurses, doctors and, of course, parents.

A heart of service expressing such energy will find joy and motivation in helping others and taking care of them. That may sometimes mean "spoiling" their clients and, at the very least, comforting them in a way that is warm and familiar. As a Peacemaker, you will be the most loved teacher, the one everyone wants to talk to, the one always welcome at the party, a group dinner or a study session. Be careful not to deplete your energy by only giving, though; of all the archetypes, Peacemakers must learn the hardest about boundaries and self-care.

As a **Perfectionist**, your heart of service will be ruled by **Metal** energy. That means you thrive when you are surrounded by beauty, order and structure. You will always choose the best quality available for every-thing and in every situation.

The Perfectionist might seem cold and distant from the outside, but the need for connection is always there. If your elemental energy is Metal, you might have an organizational or supervisory role at work. Perhaps you ensure the structure in how people deliver services and that rules, procedures and boundaries get observed. Your heart of service will be manifested in paying respect to clients and observing structure and rules: you would be perfect as a master of ceremonies or the quality manager of a five-star hotel, making sure procedures and standards are well met and your staff is perfectly trained to attend to guests.

The five elements' energies can support us in so many ways and through so many moments of our daily life. For example, in creating this chapter, I had to get in touch with my Water energy. I first had to immerse myself in deep thinking and self-reflection; that way I was able to tap into my inner self, with no interruptions or outside influences. This, in turn, allowed me to focus, nurture creative ideas and get in writing mode. In doing so, I surrounded myself with things that symbolized water for me. I created a meditation-like environment, where everything reminded me of my purpose: a lit incense stick, stones and crystals on my desk and water images on my computer screen and in my mind. And of course, it worked.

I found inspiration while taking action. I channeled my Wood energy to initiate things and fought my fears, which had long paralyzed me with writer's block. And there I was! Harnessing my motivation, I managed to take action and I wrote my notes in a beautiful brand-new notebook with a white and green cover: it depicted an image of bamboo plants, and this gave me the inspiration and strength to write.

But my main reason for writing is simply because I love doing this. I don't have to make a huge effort to find my Fire energy, as it is my essence. Fire pervades me and everything I do. I have a passion for writing, for expressing myself, just as Fire personalities love and need to do. The pen I am using for my draft (since I always handwrite my notes first) is a scented one, with purple ink. It provides pure plea-sure to the eyes, rolling onto the paper word after word, sentence after sentence and then paragraphs, pages… et voilà! What a lovely way to express my energy while enjoying the process of creating connections with the people who will read my thoughts.

I also bring Earth energy to what I am doing. That is because the under-lying reason for writing all of this is to help anyone reading and wanting or needing the energies of the five elements in their daily life. This is what I call putting your heart into the service. This is how I show the world that I care. I want my love-infused words to reach you and show you how natural and easy it is to use the energy you have inside of you for a good cause.

Last, but not least, I tap into Metal energy by surrounding myself with beauty. My source for Metallic-inspired order and structure is my cloth-ing. I am wearing my most refined silk dress as I write this, carefully respecting the guidelines our editor gave us.

So, you see? Fashion Feng Shui® and its energies pervade our world. The more we know about them, the more we can find new ways to make use of them daily. They can help us be our authentic selves, creating the life we desire by focusing on our purposes and intentions. This, in turn, makes our life, our daily life, a fulfilling one. It leads us to transform into the beautiful human beings that we all are destined to become.

Through this book, we hope you will appreciate how Fashion Feng Shui® can help you live a beautiful, intense and fulfilling life day by day. As our Evana used to say in our mission statement:

Honoring nature's five elements in all that we do, we facilitators:

Water—The Philosopher

Create holistic tools and guidelines that encourage image consultants, Feng Shui practitioners, life coaches and integrative health professionals to offer a wise, authentic, and spiritual level of counseling.

Wood—The Pioneer

Initiate change by inspiring and empowering individuals to affirm their intentions in their personal appearances in order to naturally attract what they want into their lives.

Fire—The Pleasure Seeker

Excite others about the benefits of synchronizing spirit, style and surroundings by communicating and connecting with individuals, organizations and corporations worldwide.

Earth—The Peacemaker

Nurture human beings in the exploration and expression of their innate essence, and counsel them in creating harmony and balance in both their personal appearances and their lives.

Metal—The Perfectionist

Refine and cultivate the Fashion Feng Shui® Facilitator Certification Training Course in order to support the philosophy of inclusive, holistic thought within the teachings of the image industry, Feng Shui and holistic health communities and spiritual leaders.

From the *Fashion Feng Shui® Facilitator Certification Training Coursebook*

We also want you, the reader, to realize that despite the word "fashion" being in Fashion Feng Shui®, it's never just about the clothes. It is also about the subtle yet extremely powerful energies of your clothes, accessories and environment, as well as your essence, intention and appearance. Together they affect and inform your actions and behavior.

What about you?

Do you know what energies from the five elements would best support your daily life? And on the topic of roles and dealing with others, which side of your multifaceted personality do you need to wear when dealing with your clients, guests and loved ones?

- Is it the deep/reflective one? (Water)
- Is it the competitive and encouraging one? (Wood)
- Is it the happy and playful one? (Fire)
- Is it the caring, giving one? (Earth)
- Is it the meticulous, refined one? (Metal)

Cinzia Fassetta
FFSM

Fashion Feng Shui® Master Facilitator,
Heart of Service Expert
Venice, Italy

The Heart of Service

+39 392 2945774
cinzia@theheartofservice.com
www.theheartofservice.com

Cinzia Fassetta was born and raised in Venice, Italy. She spent all her working life on the customer service side of the travel industry, gaining considerable experience in dealing with international clients.

She speaks fluent Italian, English, German and French. Her experience of Italy—its traditions, history, people and lifestyle—were the basis for establishing in 2003 StyleAndShop, her personal shopping and image consulting company, which broke new ground in Italy at the time. The experience of living, studying and working both in Italy and abroad has given Cinzia the chance to get closer to different people, nationalities and cultures.

Trained as a Fashion Feng Shui® Facilitator by Evana Maggiore in 2010, Cinzia combines her experience, personal skills and passions, while always keeping her clients' interests in mind. She offers her services to anyone wanting to upgrade an image or a wardrobe and, in so doing, transform their look and their life.

But because "You can take the girl out of hospitality, but you cannot take hospitality out of the girl," she has never forgotten where her passion really lies: welcoming people and connecting. Cinzia now applies her people skills and international experience to deliver staff training in hospitality. After authoring her book *The 7 Super Powers of the Heart*, Cinzia trained professionals in the travel industry on how to connect to guests and clients through the heart of service.

How to Choose the Right Partner
(and Get Your Dream Job, Too)

By Carmen Okabe

By now you know for sure how Fashion Feng Shui® can help you transform your look and consequently, your life.

Coming from different corners of the world—the United States, Europe and New Zealand—the previous chapters written by our Fashion Feng Shui® experts have a common message: make conscious changes in your wardrobe and your life intentions will be fulfilled!

I want to add a chapter to this book, regarding applications of Fashion Feng Shui® to human relationships and the "game" of interaction between the five elements.

Whether in our personal lives, on the quest for the right partner or in our careers, we almost always feel attraction or repulsion based on what a person looks like and the energy she or he is transmitting.

You surely need to know yourself if you are to present your best version to the world, but you also need to be prepared for each and every encounter, to always show yourself as favorably as possible.

I will give you some tips on how to quickly recognize the person standing in front of you, before you even get the chance to ask powerful questions. You might ask: What qualifies me to give you such tips?

My story

I started traveling long distance early in life. When I was 19, I was already out of my native country of Romania to attend university in Beijing, China. And since my very first trip, I developed a passion for "reading" people: analyzing their clothing, behavior and posture. This allowed me to find out where they were coming from and possibly what they were doing in life—before they even opened their mouth to reveal their language or dialect.

As a polyglot, hearing them speak afterwards was only the confirmation I needed, to see if my judgment was right or wrong. But I was guessing right 99 percent of the time.

The study abroad experience in China changed my life path dramatically. It gave me the wonderful gift of meeting an old Feng Shui master who taught me traditional Feng Shui precepts and introduced me to the great Taoist teachings. I had always dreamed of becoming an architect, and as a Feng Shui expert, I could work on the plans of a house to benefit its future inhabitants. I wished I could study more, but my life put me on another path, and for many years Feng Shui remained tucked away in a corner of my mind.

I was fascinated by Feng Shui, but what I loved most (and this love stays with me to this very day) is how you can see and understand people through the practice. Understanding how the five elements interact and how the energy reigns over us all is a great way of understanding life.

I lived half of my life in Asia, namely China and Japan. As the manager of a big company, I was responsible for hiring new people, and I got to see applications of Feng Shui at work.

I did not understand why sometimes the big boss was not deciding to hire one guy who, to me, seemed the best choice. And when I asked, he would say, "You see his birthdate? In two years he'll be running away with my clients and stealing my business!" And then he showed me the details of that guy's natal chart, its predicted interaction with the boss himself, plus the specific year this could happen.

It was intriguing to be able to "predict" the future of a relationship based on an almost mathematical formula. I decided to take a deeper look into this thing, which to me was quite a complicated science. Numbers and equations had never been my strong point, so for many years I resisted putting my knowledge into practice.

But I worked with people, all over the world, and I was still passionate about face reading. I took face reading classes, Feng Shui and BaZi classes, I spent hundreds of hours studying therapies, NLP and coaching in Asia and in Europe, and I continued to travel and analyze the people passing by.

Soon my business became influenced by my analyses, and more and more Feng Shui was integrated into the solutions I was offering to my clients. That said, it was not always easy to explain to the client what I was doing.

When I attended Evana's Fashion Feng Shui® class in 2010, it all became so easy to explain, even to someone who had no previous knowledge of Feng Shui. Not only had I found a quick tool for deep transformation, but it also became a great tool of education.

I have more than 30 years of experience coaching and consulting for private individuals and corporate teams, but I am a teacher at my core. Since 2010, I've been integrating Fashion Feng Shui® into my business. Implementing it in my clients' businesses and personal lives was a big step forward in sharing this incredible practice with them. Being able to simply explain its mechanism ensures me that the client can continue to integrate the transformation of his or her life.

So, let's see how to be prepared for any encounter, especially the one with the right person for you. Let's have a look at how interaction works and how you can recognize your soul mate.

You already know your essence, as the other chapters have given you a deep insight into your nature. You have also taken quizzes and completed exercises to discover who you are, from a Fashion Feng Shui® point of view.

You acknowledged what are, from your perspective, the most important things you cherish in life, so you are ready to set your intention for finding a life partner. At this point, I still have to push you to do another introspective exercise.

Ask yourself: **"What kind of person do I want, in my life now?"**

You might be just out of a long, traumatizing marriage or a short, passionate but abusive relationship, or maybe you are young and fresh and believe in everlasting love.

Make a wish list of how you want this person to be.

Don't be afraid to list even specific physical characteristics, but most of all, their emotional type. Pay attention to identifying how you want them to treat you. Do you want to play the dominant role in the relationship or do you prefer to be nurtured and taken care of? The vast majority of people don't think too much about these aspects when they set out to meet someone, but it's essential to envision what we want to put into and get out of a relationship.

Identify from our five elemental archetypes what type of characteristics you seek or possess. Is this an element that's compatible with your own essence or not?

How will you know this? And how can you assess compatibility? You've been waiting for the advice I promised, so here it is!

1. Learn the wheel of the five elements in the order Water—Wood—Fire—Earth—Metal. This will provide you with the generating cycle known as **Sheng**.

Based on this, you will know that a person belonging to an element preceding yours will always bring something to you in the relationship. He or she will nourish it, just as you will be the one to give more in a relationship with a person whose element comes after yours. As long as you will not feel frustrated by such a rapport, it can be a good match, creating positivity and mothering, enhancing or amplifying yourself.

Water is vital for Wood to grow.
Wood is fuel for Fire to burn.
Fire burning creates the powder of Earth.
Earth is the source of all Metal.
Out of Metal runs Water.

2. As in traditional Feng Shui, in Fashion Feng Shui® we consider the interaction between the elements and what emerges from it. Based on your answer to my question—What kind of person do you want in your life now?—you might choose a person whom your energy can control. Or the opposite—you prefer a person who will take care of you, and you're not bothered if you are "controlled."

Check the controlling cycle (known as **Kè** or **Ko**) to understand why couples stay in toxic relationships. In the controlling cycle, one person's energy weakens the other's energy, in extreme cases destroying their personality, not even intentionally, but just because it's so easy to do it.

Exactly like in nature...
Water will extinguish Fire.
Fire will melt Metal.
Metal will chop down Wood just as a lumberjack's ax cuts down trees.
Wood will break the Earth like tree roots penetrating the soil.
Earth will soak up Water and block its flow, making it mud.

Nowadays so many people are using online chats to find a mate. If you want to know when to invest yourself more in a relationship and go a step further in dating successfully, ask the person's birthdate with the full details of day, month and year.

Once you know the birthdate, you can establish if the person belongs to an element that is compatible with yours and/or if the element represents what you are looking for at this precise moment.

Tip Number 1
A person's characteristics are determined by both the ruling element of their sign as well as the element of the particular year they were born.

For instance, a Water Rabbit (like me) will be controlled by both Water and Wood.

In Fashion Feng Shui®, this represents the primary essence and the influencing essence.

And here you have the elements corresponding to the 12 animals in the Chinese zodiac:

  Water: Rat, Pig
  Wood: Tiger, Rabbit
  Fire: Snake, Horse
  Earth: Ox, Dragon, Sheep, Dog
  Metal: Monkey, Rooster

Tip Number 2

The shortcut to knowing each year's element is keeping in mind this sequence:

  All years ending in 0 and 1 are Metal.
  All years ending in 2 and 3 are Water.
  All years ending in 4 and 5 are Wood.
  All years ending in 6 and 7 are Fire.
  All years ending in 8 and 9 are Earth.

EXAMPLES:

  A person born on February 10, 1981 belongs to the Metal Rooster.
  A person born on August 28, 2003 belongs to the Water Sheep.

N.B. Pay a lot of attention and consult a Chinese calendar online for people born in January or February, as they belong to the element of the previous year.

By knowing just the birth year, you can already get an idea about the person's character. Most of all, you'll understand what the interaction will be with your own element.

And what if the person doesn't want to tell you their birthdate?

That's already a sign of their essence: the person is very probably a Water who wants to feel free to reinvent themselves or surprise you with their good looks, so you will praise them.

Anyhow, let's say you took the risk and met the guy or girl without knowing a birthdate.

This is where Fashion Feng Shui® comes in to help you: analyze the person standing before you with Fashion Feng Shui® eyes! I know you'll do it anyhow, and the first impression counts a lot. Now, instead of getting stuck on just "good-looking" and "not-so-good-looking," check out the details.

If the guy is wearing his ironed jeans with a crease and an impeccably white shirt, chances are he is Metal. Pay attention to see if he is double-checking the table setting at the restaurant and the tone of his voice, as Metals have the tendency to set rules and put order in everything, even without being asked.

If he's wearing something sporty when you meet up, even if you're out having dinner, he's probably Wood. If he tells you about winning a competition or becoming the best salesman of the year, you'll know for sure that he's Wood!

A Fire guy, besides making you feel like he wants to take you to bed for a passionate night (there's probably a bit of Fire in all guys!), gets you laughing and invites you to dance. If he's wearing a red shirt, then you know what to expect from a real Fire.

If you meet a guy looking dull and quiet in his brown sweater and outdated coat, maybe you should marry him, as Earth guys make the best husbands! He will definitely be a gentleman, opening the door for you and offering to come to repair that faucet you complained about.

The Water guy will recite poems he's written and discuss the meaning of life with you on the first date. Make sure you're equipped to deal with his daily mood swings. If you enjoy his way of being, you'll certainly never be bored, as Water is different every day.

Of course the same is valid when a guy meets a girl. I won't insist on what you have to look for in her wardrobe choices, as this whole book provides a plethora of tips on recognizing the elements.

The same rules of elemental interaction apply when you go to interview for a new job. Try to find out the birthdate of the manager or human resources officer interviewing you—make friends on the phone with his or her secretary! Then, based on the job description and the interviewer's essence, arrange your look and talk according to what would be important for his or her element. Set your intention to be in line with your essence (this will ensure that you feel at ease throughout the interview), but also to fulfill the needs of the essence of your interviewer.

Many of my clients are young people in search of "the perfect job."

After participating for two days in a Fashion Feng Shui® workshop with me, one of my clients applied for a job and got a salary package (for a junior job) that was 50 percent higher than what was standard in that company. Since then, she has been using the principles of Fashion Feng Shui® on a daily basis. She got promoted several times and is enjoying her job a lot. She has gotten lots of bonuses and free trips because she never forgets to analyze the situation from a Fashion Feng Shui® point of view before any important meeting.

Here's a word from her: "Hello, Carmen! I wanted to thank you one more time for the opportunity you gave me to learn about Fashion Feng

Shui®! I used all the information you shared with me and today I received a positive answer from a multinational company, with such a generous offer, I was never even dreaming about! At the interview, I managed to do some mirroring with the manager, but mostly, I used your tips for the non-verbal communication, and it worked! I am so delighted with the result, that I will study FFS even deeper. Thanks again, you are the best!"

Fashion Feng Shui® can really change your life, and the sooner you learn about elemental interaction, the better you will be prepared for any challenge life can bring you!

I love working with people, and helping them transform quickly won me the nickname of Transformation Wizard. Don't hesitate to contact me to see what my magic wand can do for you!

I hope you've enjoyed our book and are now ready to enter a new dimension on your life path, equipped with all the information we've offered you.

Remember that clothes are our most intimate environment, and it's up to us to decide how well and how high we set our intentions in the quest for happiness, love and prosperity! Dressing with intention makes us focus on our plans and helps us be conscious of our decisions.

Let Fashion Feng Shui® be part of your daily life and prosperity will follow!

Carmen Okabe
FFSM

Fashion Feng Shui® Master Facilitator,
"Transformation Wizard"
Lausanne, Switzerland and
Beijing, China

Swiss Image Institute

+41 798 39 39 81
carmen@carmenokabe.ch
www.swissimageinstitute.com
www.carmenokabe.ch

Carmen Okabe was born in Romania to parents of Turkish and Hungarian descent. She studied in China and got married in Japan, where she lived before going on to live in France, Turkey, China (again), Belgium and Romania (again). She is now based in Switzerland, where she runs the Swiss Image Institute and the Swiss Institute for Alternative Medicines (ISMED).

Carmen is who she is today thanks to the multitude of cultures she has lived in, along with her passion for studying human nature and finding ways to improve its outer and inner beauty. Her quest to offer full-package solutions for individuals seeking positive transformation is motivated by Carmen's own personal tao, in search of balance. She has been transformed by various encounters with great therapists, opportunities to follow Feng Shui masters, as well as countless business experiences.

Holding a BA in Oriental languages and a Master's degree in Japanese Management, Carmen is a member of the Association of Image Consultants International and former vice president of education of the

AICI France chapter. Carmen studied face reading in Japan, traditional Feng Shui in China, Fashion Feng Shui® with Evana Maggiore in the U.S., Aesthetic Fengshui in France, international etiquette and protocol in Belgium and hypnosis and NLP in Switzerland. She is passionate about human design and has developed her own coaching method uniting all of these interests.

For nine years, Carmen has served as publisher of the professional beauty magazine *Les Nouvelles Esthétiques*. She also created Estetik TV, a channel dedicated to the world of image. She has over 25 years of experience in management, marketing and media, personal branding and marketing with heart. She is a certified executive coach, a Transformation Game facilitator, a Mind Mapping licensed instructor, and an international speaker and author. For over 15 years, Carmen has appeared as a beauty and image industry expert in dozens of programs for various TV channels, and she has written several books and manuals.

She believes that always being curious and reinventing yourself—thus evolving and filling in the missing parts—is the key to happiness and success. Her own power of transformation and the impact she has on her clients has earned her the nickname "Transformation Wizard."

Speaking fluently Chinese, Japanese, Turkish, English, French, Italian, Spanish and Romanian, Carmen gives conferences and classes on image transformation, international etiquette and personal grooming, personal branding, marketing, Fashion Feng Shui®, Mind Mapping and home management. She acts as a business consultant all over the world.

In 2012 and 2014, the Chinese government conferred on her the title of Ambassador of Feng Shui Culture to the World, recognizing her contribution to helping spread appreciation for the art of placement outside Asia.

Carmen feels best when creating and taking charge, so she regularly organizes international symposiums on Feng Shui, astrology, beauty, health and image.

She is the initiator and editor of this book.

Fashion Feng Shui®
Create Closet Harmony, Live Your Best Life™

Fashion Feng Shui® stands out from other image practices because it looks at us as whole people. Our clothing choices are as individual as our fingerprints, and our clothing is our most intimate environment. By combining mind, body and soul, Fashion Feng Shui® empowers us to find our unique style so we have confidence in wearing whatever works for us. Fashion Feng Shui® evolves with us as we practice it, so our appearance, desires and lifestyle will always be harmoniously balanced through our closet choices.

In addition to our annual online Facilitator Certification Training Course (scheduled each fall), we have offerings for individual personal enrichment in the form of the Transform Your Look & Life™ Workshop and the Dress For Your Dreams™ e-course. For those in the corporate market, the most recent addition to our repertoire is the much-praised Work Your Element™ Business Seminar, which adapts Fashion Feng Shui® principles for professionals who consult in a business setting.

Two levels of certification

Fashion Feng Shui® Facilitators (FFSF) are individuals who have successfully completed our 15-week Facilitator Certification Training Course (FCT). They have been awarded the annually renewable rights to offer Fashion Feng Shui® consultations and seminars to clients. Fashion  Feng Shui® Facilitators are designated by the professional credentials of "FFSF" after their names. To find a Fashion Feng Shui® Facilitator near you, please visit fashionfengshui.com.

Fashion Feng Shui® Master Facilitators (FFSM) are highly-qualified licensed Fashion Feng Shui® Facilitators who have been awarded the annually renewable rights to offer Fashion Feng Shui® consultations and seminars to clients as well as to professionally train and certify new Fashion Feng Shui® Facilitators. Fashion Feng Shui® Master Facilitators are designated by the professional credentials of "FFSM" after their names.

Virtual course offerings

Dress for Your Dreams™

This brilliant e-course shows you how to dress for your dreams—step by step, using a mixture of explanation, photos and video. Delivered daily to your inbox in 12 simple stages, it gives you the time and the guidance to implement and see the results for yourself.
Visit dressforyourdreams.com to sign up.

Transform Your Look & Life™ Workshop

Are your clothes speaking your truth? Does every garment express your true magnificence—physically, mentally and spiritually? Does your attire affirm your desires so that you will naturally attract them into your life? On this five-week journey of self-discovery, you learn how to make conscious clothing choices that fulfill your spirit, flatter your appearance, function for your lifestyle and fortify you to attract your desires.
Visit fashionfengshui.com to see our schedule of upcoming sessions.

Facilitator Certification Training Course

Innovate or expand your consulting business by joining our international network of Fashion Feng Shui® Facilitators. Discover how our five-element theory provides harmony and balance in our clothing, and how it can help your clients make clothing choices that embrace their mind, body and soul. Over the course of 15 weeks, you learn to select colors, patterns, textures, fabrics and style lines that reflect your clients' authentic selves and help them get what they want.

Visit fashionfengshui.com to see our schedule of upcoming sessions.

WORK YOUR ELEMENT™

Business Success Your Way

Work Your Element™ Business Seminar

Work Your Element™ takes the principles of Fashion Feng Shui® to the workplace, applying our five-element theory to businesses and corporate situations. Understanding and utilizing the positive energy of the elements can enhance business relationships, create productive flow, increase retention of good people, enable them to excel as individuals and teams, and utilize their skill base in work environments.

Visit workyourelement.com for more information.

Andrew Maggiore
Director

Fashion Feng Shui International
13 Wheeling Avenue
Woburn, MA 01801
USA

+1 781.718.2008
andrew@fashionfengshui.com
www.fashionfengshui.com

For information on our offerings, please contact info@fashionfenghsui.com or call Andrew. You can also find us on Facebook, Twitter and Instagram.

NAMASTE